AF240863

THE POWER OF BABIES
On the trails of the "Wi-Fi babies"

Daniel Rousseau

THE POWER OF BABIES
On the trails of the "Wi-Fi babies"

Max Milo

Max Milo Editions

Collection Essais-Documents, Paris, 2023

www.maxmilo.com

ISBN : 978-2-315-01102-5

Preface by Céline Raphaël

Elise, a young woman wounded by life, recently wrote to me about how the neglect she suffered as a child had shattered her life. Her mother's lack of interest in her, the unspoken words, this maternal refusal of a real connection with her daughter made her a woman without an image. A hologram. Worse, a wandering ghost. In any case, this is how she felt, and when it comes to suffering, one must start from the feeling, recognize it rather than judge it or deny it in the name of reason.

This wounded young child had no one to reach out to. No network she could hack into, no power source detected within reach, neither in family nor in friends. And a deep depression began to eat away at her body, gorging itself on loneliness and self-pity. A soul so bruised that it gradually fell asleep so as not to suffer anymore. Like Sleeping Beauty, waiting for the Prince Charming who would reach out to her to get her out of her torpor. Fortunately, human beings are often resilient, their soul is tenacious. It can be put on standby but never dies. It is difficult to completely destroy a person's emotional sensors. There is always a small signal. And for Elise, this fragile little signal is still struggling to detect an open and friendly communication network, without abstruse passwords, to connect to. She reaches out to us, groping in the dark. If she had met Dr. Rousseau earlier, she would have found her WiFi terminal, human, benevolent, humble and wise.

I met Dr. Daniel Rousseau shortly after I began my medical internship. I had promised myself to devote part of my life to the fight against child abuse and I felt that it was the right time. I had contacted Dr. Anne Tursz, a pediatrician and epidemiologist at INSERM and she introduced me to Daniel. Together, we embarked on this fight, this cause that was so dear to all three of us. We decided to fight to make child abuse in France everyone's concern, in order to see a decrease in the number of victims and the long term consequences that it causes. Abuse is a tsunami that destroys everything in its path and shatters the future of the children it strikes.

At present, in France, if "excessive" abuse, physical, sexual, psychological, is fairly well identified as such, it must be noted that less blatant abuse, such as neglect, is still not taken seriously and is less identified than the others. Neglect occurs whenever the "normal" attachment between parent and child is prevented. It can be linked to a marital conflict that mobilizes the couple's energy, thus abandoning the child. It can be linked to a parental psychiatric pathology, often a depression of the mother, who is then unable to take care of herself and therefore of her child. Neglect can also be a consequence of a chronic pathology, physical or mental of the child. In the latter case, the child imagined, dreamed of, projected in the parents' imagination during the entire pregnancy finally appears "non-conform" to this idyllic image. The fragile parent then runs the risk of not being able to achieve the attachment that is essential for the development of his or her child. A sort of denial of parenthood that sets in more or less insidiously.

And make no mistake about it: everyone is affected. Like physical, psychological and sexual abuse, neglect is not limited to poor or marginal families. They are hidden everywhere, behind the walls of middle-class houses as well as behind those of the most modest dwellings, as I told my own story in *La Démesure*[1]. The impossibility of loving, of becoming attached to, of connecting properly with one's

---

1. RAPHAËL (Céline), *La Démesure*, Paris, Max Milo, 2013.

child, is not proportional to the solvency of the bank account. In any case, the consequences can be terrible. One does not repair a deep emotional scar with a mountain of fluff.

In order to help these neglected children, we face a major obstacle, as Dr. Rousseau so well tells us: the idea that the family is "naturally good". And this utopian belief wreaks havoc on the hearts of children. In the name of this idea, child protection services try to remove children from their families as late as possible and only in cases of serious and documented neglect, while constantly trying to re-establish the relationship between the child and his or her parents with a view to returning the child to the parental home. This is no doubt done with good intentions. However, all too often, the parental network is severely blurred or of very poor quality, and this is irreversible. The child will never be able to detect a secure connection and flourish within the family.

For a long time, it was thought that small children did not really feel conscious pain. So, in the hospital, we pricked without any other form of trial, we even operated sometimes without any anesthesia! Things have changed in this area. Pain in young children is understood, admitted and tried to be fought. Just like that pain that "didn't exist", the need for a stable and secure attachment of a baby is not yet taken seriously. We imagine that the plasticity of infants is almost infinite. After all, if his mother fails, he has his father, an uncle, an aunt, the nanny, a neighbor, even... television. Eventually, this little man will find something to suit him." Life is hard for everyone, you have to suffer... Here again, we are mistaken. If the cerebral and sentimental plasticity of the child is real, as this book demonstrates, it has its limits and a child abandoned for too long risks fading away little by little to wander, like a spectre, in a world of solitude from which he will not come out unscathed.

Daniel Rousseau is a born storyteller. He knows how to give life to these children's stories, so singular and so universal. Rather than using abstract rhetoric, he has chosen to take the shortcut that speaks for itself: "WiFi baby". He uses a digital metaphor: the relationship between the baby and its parents is likened to a wireless connection, more or less strong, more or less free. The technical analogy does not mean that the child is equated with a machine - it allows us to put words on feelings and behaviors. It is not an exercise in style but a desire to better define the targets and means of healing action. Doctor Rousseau manages to demonstrate that the essential thing is to act in time by removing the child, if possible temporarily, but if necessary permanently, from a defective parental network, to offer him the possibility of coming into contact with adults, mothering people, foster mothers, psychologists, a world that is much more reassuring for him. The child knows better than you or me which are the best and healthiest "adult WiFi" terminals, and he will be able to detect them if he is offered the possibility to be in a well-covered geographical area.

The phenomenon of WiFi babies that Daniel Rousseau narrates is in my opinion universal. His observations are so accurate and practical that they have allowed me to reinterpret or better unders- tand the situations I encounter every day in the hospital in various pediatric departments. Three stories particularly struck me.

Foodil is an 8 year old boy with Down Syndrome. Five minutes after his birth, his mother loses her sight without any cause, preventing her from taking care of her newborn. She wanders in a world of darkness, lost, unable to get in touch with him. Fortunately, Foodil's father is very present. Strong and serene, or at least giving this impression by dint of his courage, he takes care of his son, offering him a secure and safe network. And gradually, by listening to her son's babbling, his bursts of laughter, and sometimes his tears, Foodil's mother will emerge from this long tunnel of sadness and darkness. A long road towards the acceptance of the difference of her son. After two years, she regained her sight and discovered her child through touch and sight. Foodil did not reject her, on the contrary. He welcomed her, he forgave her. As if he had understood the suffering of his mother. As if he knew, deep down, that she had loved him from the beginning but had not known how to connect with him.

I also remember Tania. Tania is 13 years old. She is a perfectly normal little girl, surrounded by her loving parents, ideally connected to them until the age of 1. Then she couldn't hold her head anymore. And then she couldn't sit up. One by one, the muscles in her body gave up on her, due to leukodystrophy. She didn't babble anymore. She didn't laugh anymore. Soon, only her intense eyes were left to express the immensity of her feelings and sensations. Her mom managed to maintain a good quality connection with her. They talked for hours through their eyes and Tania fought hard to maintain this connection. But for her dad, it was not so simple. He loved his daughter. It is a certainty. But the shock of the announcement, the intrusion of this disease in their life was too hard to handle. He looked away. He broke the connection. And then he left, far away, coming back from time to time, according to Tania's hospitalizations in intensive care, at each announcement of an imminent death. But during their meetings, if he made an effort to get in touch with his daughter, by the look, by the touch, his embarrassment was so palpable that this time, it was Tania who did not look at him anymore. She felt his trouble and could not bear it. Then, like the Sleeping Beauty, she gave the illusion of a deep sleep when her father was in the room and she woke up when her mother took over.

And then there is Amara. Amara is 3 years old and has a twin of the same age. He is affected by one of those degenerative pathologies so unfair. He can no longer make a single movement. Only his eyes, piercing, testify of his will to live, despite everything. His twin brother is "healthy". He is a mischievous little boy who runs around. The good side of the mirror. His mom and dad gradually turned away from Amara to focus on his brother. They forgot about the sick Amara and felt soothed by his healthy double. In his little bed, few toys, few stuffed animals. No mother in the room. Amara quickly realized, however, that the nurse, the nurse's aide, the intern, the doctor were looking at him with great interest and affection. They were obviously trying to communicate with him. Through smiles, through touch.

And Amara understood that this is what he was missing at home. So the stays at home became shorter and shorter. And each time, an apnea that was too long brought him back home. More and more often. It was as if the lack of connection with his parents was suffocating him and that he needed this little hospital room, the attention of the caregivers to find a breath of oxygen. A breath of life.

Life triumphs where it is not always expected, such is the subject of Daniel Rousseau's beautiful book. A very simple and human book, rich in teachings, which has the courage to debunk the myth of the importance of biological parents to remind us that the baby is above all a human being, ready to embrace this world and to act in it, as long as we do not turn our backs on him.

Preamble

Early childhood remains an unknown land, even though we have all been there for a long time.

Early childhood is a world of gentle or violent, but fleeting emotions, whose perception, acute at this age, slowly fades. Indeed, when the time comes for feelings, words and memories, these are written in bold letters on the parchment of life, covering the delicate primordial weft of emotions, like a palimpsest.

We all went through this early childhood, without looking at the landscapes and without fixing the images, probably too preoccupied as we were with simply living and surviving. In the light luggage of our childhoods, we keep very few tangible memories of this moving journey, and words are lacking to describe the panorama.

May the itinerary of this book offer some perspectives, just as a steep and horizonless mountain road can, through sudden gaps in the vegetation, reveal to us peaks and abysses. Then, like curious young children raised on the tip of their feet, we stretch our necks to observe what usually remains invisible to our eyes and impenetrable to our understanding.

But how to enter this forgotten world?

We still have a chance: if babies do not speak, they nevertheless trade with their fellow human beings through the power of their emotions. They address them to us with energy and deposit them in us where they take root if we pay attention to them. To feel them, to accept them, to share them, to respond to them is the best way to access the understanding of the sensitive and intense universe of babies. Babies surprise and overwhelm you with their emotions. You have to accept to be led by them.

Let's follow those of little Laura who will give us a glimpse of some of the perspectives opened in this book.

First perspective:
the baby powerfully trades in emotions

While I was attending a very serious meeting at the children's home[2], unusual scents tickled my attention. Like Captain Haddock's plaster, the question of where this scent came from stuck in my brain and then invaded my thoughts and I couldn't get rid of it.

They were my hands. My palms and fingers smelled of orange. It was curious. The mystery of my scented hands soon became heady.

Reduced to the state of an absent-minded dunce, I explained in a low voice my perplexity and my embarrassing question to my neighbor, who opened her eyes in astonishment and did not know what to answer to such a crazy information. The child psychiatrist is surprised to have hands that smell like orange peel. A little bit crazy!

---

2. The children who pass through these pages have been taken in a nursery of a children's home. These are permanent care facilities for babies and young children entrusted to the Child Welfare Services by judicial decision in most cases, and by the parents themselves in a very small proportion.

Suddenly it was an illumination. It was little Laura who had slipped into my head through this olfactory sensation and who was no longer leaving. I discovered myself, in spite of myself, haunted by this child.

Laura and I had run into each other in the hallway not ten minutes ago. I didn't know her. She had never seen me. We were stuck in the traffic jam of meal carts that were being wheeled from the kitchen to the various dining rooms. Sitting on top of one of them, enthroned among the fruit, she tried to catch my attention without daring to look at me. She then handed me a ball. I accepted her gesture and received this gift. "Thank you! I don't know you! What is your name?" She lowered her head.

Her educator replied, "It's Laura, she's two and a half years old, she arrived at the home only a few days ago."

Like Laura, babies have the power to creep into our thoughts without our knowledge by bombarding us with their emotions.

Second perspective:
a baby's love for its parents is not unconditional

I gave Laura her ball back and she offered it to me again. The dislocation of the lunch cart traffic jam interrupted our game. The little girl put the orange back in the fruit basket. I got a sneaky peek.

Her educator told me that Laura was a plaster child. Since her admission, she had adapted very quickly to the nursery and asked to be held by everyone she met. She never asked for her parents and when her mother wanted to talk to her on the phone, Laura would reach out, turn her back to the educator who offered her the phone and nod "no".

With her daughter, this mother had alternated coercive attitudes and profound disinterest. She left her tied up in her stroller the whole day. And she didn't mind making her skip lunch when she forgot to go shopping.

Laura quickly called her educator "mom" and hugged her head tenderly between her little arms. This shows that a child's love for his parents is not unconditional. Laura had also shown me this by her emotional search for a stranger, me in this case, and by the concern she caused me as a result.

Let me explain.

The little man is powerless to live alone and from his first moments of life he is able to arouse the empathy of humans by seeking to connect to the best emotional terminals at his disposal where he projects his emotions. A baby can only survive and exist if it is embedded in the head and heart of a reliable adult who will know how to care for it. If he does not find this vital availability from his parents, he will turn to other humans. This is what Laura had done and she had managed to move me in a few seconds as she had done before with my colleagues.

Laura was in danger at her mother's house, in chaos, lack of care, permanent insecurity and a climate of terror most of the time. Her older brother and sister told us quickly and frighteningly about the "blue stick" that had its place on the dining room dresser. Laura found the emotional responses and attention she was missing from the nursery professionals. She very quickly chose to attach herself to reassuring strangers rather than to her parents, who were unsuitable and dangerous.

Perspective Three:
Infants make discriminatory affective choices

I now call these little ones, who connect emotionally to the most secure adults around them, WiFi babies[3] by analogy with the portable

---

3. WiFi - Wireless Fidelity - is to fast Internet what 3G or 4G is to cell phone, except that you choose your connection point according to the access codes you know and the quality of the signal of the available *Hot Spots*. You can use Internet on your personal box in WiFi while your teenagers are connected on the public *Hot Spots* of the neighbors.

electronic devices that discriminately scan the surrounding digital terminals in search of the best connection point.

But it took me twenty years of observation to discover and understand that this phenomenon, which can be observed in children, was first and foremost an early skill of the baby, and that it is exercised from the first day of its life. It is therefore not a behavior that is acquired over time, quite the contrary, since this aptitude withers and disappears quite quickly if the infant does not find a quality connection available. In these severe cases, the baby may permanently lose this innate skill because it needs to be recognized, welcomed, supported, nourished and enriched by the environment in order to flourish.

From the very beginning of my work in the children's home in Angers, young children put me on this track by behaviors and remarks that confused me a lot. For example, during parental visits, some children did not go towards their parents, but instead distanced themselves and sought the protection of their educators. This went against the common belief that children suffer systematically from being separated from their families. I discovered that this was far from always being the case with maladjusted, sick or violent parents. Surprised by these observations, I found myself lost, without any reference points, nor any help in what I had learned during my studies, where I had been taught respect for parental authority, the duty of professional neutrality and the necessary emotional distance. Nevertheless, I followed the path that these children showed me without knowing where it would lead me. They allowed me to understand little by little the phenomenon of selective affective connections which turned out to be independent of the family geography.

This observation also contradicted the common perception of babies as dependent, passive, and slow to become aware of themselves and the world, because they actually have the ability to develop subtle and complex behaviors to attract the attention, interest, and affection of others from the first hours of life. This is a vital necessity. It was a real surprise to discover that babies were gifted with a certain degree of autonomy, with the limits imposed by their dependence on others, in their search for reliable emotional support. This book will therefore also tell the story of how babies communicate with grown-ups and how they seek a place with them.

All babies function on this mode of affective search for the best quality, or sufficient quality, but in the majority of cases, that is to say when the parents are attentive to their child, the discriminative dimension of this phenomenon is not perceptible since the child normally attaches to them. This is why we are under the illusion that emotional attachment to parents is a logical and natural process.

The perception and the description of this universal phenomenon, the discriminative affective research of the infant, were thus made possible only by the contribution of several very particular conditions during the observation of these babies.

They lived apart from their parents and were welcomed in a social nursery where attention to the children's well-being was a priority, which offered them a quality emotional alternative. Their parents nevertheless came regularly to spend time with them during visits in the presence of an educator and a psychologist. These infants had the freedom to explore the quality of the affective connections in the family network - where the parental deficiencies that had motivated their placement did not fail to manifest themselves - while nevertheless having the guarantee of finding constant and reassuring substitute affective support from their educators. It was therefore easy to observe over the long term any changes in the affective behaviours adopted by these babies towards their parents or their educators.

Fourth perspective:
the baby does not believe in the biological link

It is this unique device that has allowed the observation of the still unknown phenomenon of the affective discrimination of babies. There are many lessons to be learned about the formation of the first human bonds, but the most unexpected conclusion is that for the child the notions of "biological bond or legal bond" do not exist. For a baby, who can only survive in total dependence on others, the only question that is worthwhile is to be taken care of in an adapted and reassuring way by another human, apart from any other consideration.

A baby doesn't care about race, gender, origin or creed when choosing an attachment figure. The only thing that matters to him is the quality of the affective response he receives.

1 - WHY DID YOU LEAVE ME ALONE?

Jules, 5 years old,
selective affective connection teacher

Jules, 5 years old, was my first teacher in selective emotional connection. It was a time when the Internet was still a curiosity and wireless connections did not exist.

The children's judge had ordered Jules to be placed in a children's home. His father had severe psychiatric problems. He had assaulted Jules' older sister while delirious and had been hospitalized. He now appeared to be slowed down by medication. The judge, informed of his mental disorders, had nevertheless authorized him to visit his son and it had been considered judicious that the young child psychiatrist that I was still, fresh from the faculty, was present at this meeting organized at the children's home.

The child did not know me very well, I had only seen him once before. The visit went on laboriously. I had the feeling of a mutual reserve between the father and the child.

The child did not go to his father and the father was not very active in going to his son. How could a father and child not be happy to be reunited after a few weeks of separation? To me, the situation was getting heavy. I tried a few maneuvers to facilitate the dialogue, proposing to the child to tell him about the school, the home, his hobbies and inviting the father to reassure him about his absence, his condition and to take an interest in his son. Without success. Each one remained on his own. And I saw my lamentable attempt to reconnect the child with his father fail.

I had the naive idea that it was my presence - I was a stranger to the family - that hindered the expression of their affection. So I had the idea to slip away discreetly and leave them alone, hoping that this would free their emotional spontaneity.

I offered Jules the opportunity to draw a picture and used the excuse of an urgent job to leave my office and leave them between them, the door ajar. I went to wait in the nearby secretariat, within earshot. I tried to concentrate on some mail to write, but the persistent silence coming from the next room overrode the sound environment, the clatter of the typewriters and the conversation of the secretaries. It was a painful silence that clouded my thinking. Although we didn't know each other very well, Jules, from a distance, imposed himself on my mind and caused me concern.

I went back to them. Jules was staring at the door and seemed to be waiting for me. His father remained motionless and distant. A warm goodbye and he left.

The ten words that changed my perception of childhood

The child suddenly asked me: "Why did you leave me alone? I was afraid with Daddy!"

I realized that day that Jules felt safer with an adult he didn't know than with his own father. I also admitted that Jules had aroused a certain concern in me that I didn't yet know how to name, even though we had no connection. Can a child feel alienated from his parents and confide in a stranger? If so, this was in total contradiction with everything I had been taught in college about the deontological respect of parental authority and family law. And in complete opposition to everything that was conveyed in socio-educational and social work circles: not getting attached to children and refusing any emotional relationship for fear of usurping the place of the parents (official version), or having to manage the emotional complications of a reciprocal attachment when the child leaves (practical version)! Indeed, these children sometimes have complicated backgrounds with successive placements, which causes emotional ruptures that are certainly difficult to negotiate for them, but also for the professionals who have taken them in.

I thus discovered how much, unbeknownst to me, my understanding of the world of childhood and the family was then parasitized by the dominant and widespread discourse that a little one always wanted to be with his parents and that it was necessary to support their role as parents at all costs in the interest of the child. Another variant of this discourse is that the child needs his parents more than anything else and that they must therefore be defended at all costs. This can lead to the silly syllogism that follows when the family is failing: protect the child by protecting the parents - who do not protect the child. However, the attitude and behavior of some children show the opposite when they seek to avoid contact with their parents and find reassurance from professionals. In order to identify this position of the child, it is necessary to be open to such an eventuality and to accept to recognize it.

At the time, I had not yet practiced this look and was instead trained to respond to these children, and thus to Jules, using the usual normative discourse, so often served and re-served to children, which consists of excusing the parents by giving a reassuring explanation or a false hope to the child, or even advising him to forget what he has seen or felt.

According to the logic of my medical training and the canons of social work thinking, I should have replied to Jules, the voice docto-

1 - Why did you leave me alone?

ring and condescending, "Your father loves you, you are worried about him being sick, but you don't have to be afraid of him."

Just as I heard the other children say, "It's true, your mother didn't come to see you, but she's thinking about you. She didn't call? It's because she doesn't have a phone plan anymore." "Did your parents forget your birthday? They probably have too much to worry about right now." "Did your father get angry and break everything? But it's because he was drunk, it's the alcohol's fault." "Did your parents get into a fight? It's because they have too many problems, don't worry, you should think about something else." "Your dad got stabbed at the carnival? Was it your mom's boyfriend who did that to him? And he went with you to the hospital walking with the knife stuck in his stomach? Do you know that it's not good to tell lies in front of your classmates to scare them and show off[4]!"

"Why did you leave me alone? I was scared with Dad!"

Jules' reflection had touched and unsettled me. So I refrained from the usual nonsense. Instead, I told him that when his father came back, there would always be an adult from the home, an educator, a psychologist or myself, to be present at his side. I took Jules back to his educators. In the corridor, he took my hand and shook three fingers of his right hand very hard. My answer and his gesture of assent had put me outside the rules of benevolent neutrality advocated in my professional practice and had led me down side roads without map or compass. But since then, I have never regretted having taken and explored them.

---

4. A funny anecdote, with the hindsight of time, which happened to a 4 years old boy, placed in the children's home. He had told the story of "his weekend" to the class on Monday morning. His teacher didn't believe him and summoned the educators to reprimand him in front of witnesses and warn him not to tell any more stories to his classmates. Convincing the children's judge that weekend outings were not desirable in these conditions was difficult, as the father did not want to file a complaint for obscure reasons. The police had therefore had no knowledge of the aggression, although it was real, as the person concerned confirmed to us later. The word of the children is always suspect.

I have never forgotten this lesson from a 5 year old.

Afterwards, I remained sensitive and attentive to this double observation that is difficult to admit: a child can go outside the family circle to seek emotional, physical or psychological security and be more concerned about a stranger than about his own parents.

Marc and the coffee maker

I remember Marc before he came to the children's home. He was 7 years old. He lived alone with his mother, a former teacher who had triggered a delusional psychosis. She lived in a world of her own, but was still able, on certain days, to adapt to some of the concrete demands of daily life, to run three errands, to prepare a semblance of a meal. She spent her days lost in crazy writing. They lived in the last apartment still occupied in a tower promised to be demolished, the execution of which was constantly postponed, a fascinating spectacle in perspective, because of the impossibility of making them leave the premises. The building was deserted but the mother, subject to a delusion of persecution, refused all offers of relocation. The hygiene of the apartment was deplorable. Marc did not smell good. At night, his mother wandered the streets, soliloquizing or insulting invisible interlocutors while visiting the garbage cans. Marc accompanied her, a discreet little nocturnal presence in the urban desert, which intrigued a police patrol. This is what finally accelerated his placement.

Marc was a bright child who had invested a lot of time in school where caring adults had taken an interest in him. He was always glued to his teacher and sought her attention by producing excellent work. Adults would analyze the situation by saying that he was deficient in affection, as if it were a vitamin or iron deficiency, and that a good dose of daily attention would take care of it. This was a misunderstanding of two things. The first is that for a child - but passionate lovers experience this too - love is not a commodity that

1 - Why did you leave me alone?

can be shared by the piece, by the cut, by the bag, by the dose, by the unit of time, temperature, weight, length or volume. For thus measured, it is only affection, attention, benevolence, but not love, which contains each of these dimensions but exceeds them all by its absolute character.

The second thing is that school does not take up all the hours of a day, nor all the days of a week, nor all the months of a year. Life was difficult with this mother who was overwhelmed by her delusional thoughts, inaccessible to sensible conversation, and who refused all offers of care. For her, it was the others who were crazy.

So, before school, after school, Marc spent his time at the little bar across the street with Mr. Victor, the café owner. Accustomed to doing many things on his own, to surviving alone in the adult world, Marc was bold with customers and came across as a shameless child. But Mr. Victor, who understood the child's loneliness, tolerated him as best he could - social services were slow to make a decision about placement. He didn't allow himself to refuse the messy, zealous and eager help of the child who cleared the barely finished glasses, spoke loudly and without restraint, was on first-name terms with the clientele, asked for tips and meddled in everything. In any case, if he had kicked Marc out of the restaurant, he would have gone back in through the window. Mark lived as a squatter in Mr. Victor's house. It is this characteristic that I will later find in babies who are capable of selective affective connections: they manage to occupy adult brains that are not their parents', when the adults they meet are receptive and attentive to them.

Louise and Luc are afraid of their parents

When I started working in the nursery, another story, that of Louise and Luc, 4 years old and 3 years old, reinforced my observation that children in danger can show mistrust towards their parents and go towards foreign adults to seek security. This second characteristic that I observe in babies is easier to understand and to conceive in older children. It may still be hard for you to accept that this is the case with babies.

To say that Louise and Luc's mother was not easy to live with would be an understatement. The family worker who accompanied them on weekly outings to the home was not very reassured herself. She had learned not to upset this woman to protect the children from her unpredictable mood swings and thunderous tantrums. But she didn't always succeed. She told us that once, when their mother couldn't find her new kitten in the apartment, she went into an uncontrollable rage, accusing the children of some misdeed. She ordered them to sit on the couch and not to move until the young animal was back. The family worker had to do the same and was stuck with the children, sitting the whole afternoon three to a side in two cramped seats, until Mr. Cat came out of his closet after his nap. This mother terrorized her children and professionals, and gave them less consideration than her pet.

That was before I knew their father.

I had summoned Louise and Luc's parents to an interview at the children's home. I took them into the consultation room, which was furnished, on its diagonal axis, with a small table and a chair for the doctor, and two comfortable chairs opposite, at a relative distance. It was spacious, with plenty of room to move around. A few games and toys were laid out on a carpet in one corner, on the other diagonal, halfway between the parents and the consultant. An educator brought the children into the room. They paused when they saw their father, I noticed a sort of fleeting twitch in Luc's face, and then they hugged their parents. Then, to my surprise, they made no attempt to explore the games, standing almost studiously by the visitors. I was surprised, knowing Louis' great difficulty in staying in place and his incessant agitation. Motus and mouths sewn, wise as images, two children of wax. All four were facing me.

Sitting behind my small desk, I began the interview, in order to relax the atmosphere, with a few banalities about my satisfaction that they had come to exchange and about the good looks of the children.

1 - Why did you leave me alone?

During these meetings, I always try to gather the parents' feelings on the reasons for the placement, their level of understanding of its necessity and their appreciation of the child's evolution. This is an exercise that worried me at the beginning, imagining the possible hostile reactions of parents who had had their children taken away. Experience has shown me that this behavioral pattern is marginal and that, on the contrary, in the vast majority of cases, these battered parents are grateful that their children are being cared for and that they are being kept informed.

It is in this calm spirit that I also approached this appointment, with nevertheless two small flashes in a corner of my thoughts: wax children and a problematic cat.

Louise and Luc's parents were as calm and cold as the sea in the eye of a cyclone when it takes on a dark oil hue, under the cover of a black and motionless sky. No sound, no breath, not even the sound of the surf. Terse answers without apparent emotion. Not very long-winded despite the stakes of the situation. But the interview quickly got out of hand for a futile pretext.

They stood up in unison and began to yell in a discordant duet, each with a dissonant score. I will always remember this astonishing scene of two parents yelling at each other and cursing at me without even listening to or echoing each other. In reaction to the increasing volume of sound, I saw two little wax statues move in secret, away from their parents, pass by the playground without stopping and go along the wall to take refuge imperceptibly behind me. In search of a protective haven from the impending hurricane, they had used me as a breakwater for shelter. Our position was submerged by the successive waves of a violent and aggressive verbal flood which redoubled in front of the spectacle of the two runaways who had dared to seek refuge outside the parental bosom. The proof that the nursery was indeed a service of child thieves and that, in addition, they were turning them against their legal ascendants. The screaming departure of the parents was accompanied by death threats against me but put an end to this painful episode.

We learned that the children had had the same experience in court. Louise and Luc had witnessed a violent outburst by their parents who, shouting, had insulted and promised the worst to the children's judge who was supposed to be the embodiment of the law and to protect them from these excesses. The judge threatened to refer them to the prosecutor, without much effect.

As a result of these events, we understood why Luke was throwing tantrum after tantrum. In his eyes and in his cries, there were tears of despair and aggressive fury. He blinked like a flashing light, depending on whether he experienced himself as the terrified child or identified with the terrifying father. Louise also oscillated in contradictory affective movements towards her educators, asking for reassurance and comfort one moment, only to sink a little later into aggressiveness and opposition, and then return to be comforted. They both alternated in their emotional connections between the exhausting short-circuit of being both fascinated victims and frightening monsters, staying tuned to the anguishing spectacle imposed by these terrible parents. But if they wished to rest at a distance from this frightening universe in the more reassuring arms of their educators, they saw themselves exposed to another danger, having seen their parents repeatedly attack this haven in principle protected. No refuge could be guaranteed to them.

Children choose guardians who are not always their parents

Children suffering from very difficult parents look for comforting external supports that are sometimes difficult to provide.

In my previous book[5], on the stories of children from the children's home in Angers, I reread in Stéphane's story "this particular episode,

---

5. *Big People are really stupid : what distressed children teach us*, Paris, Max Milo, 2013.

from which I learned a lot [...] where this little hand slipped stealthily and secretly to a professional rather than to his parents had then enlightened us on Stéphane's deep insecurity in front of them and on the fact that he did not recognize them as tutelary adults." Today, in the aftermath, fifteen years later, I can conclude that I had already become aware of the phenomenon of selective affective connections, but that I did not yet know how to give them a name. And if I had then described them in a limpid way, this example testifies to it, I was still very far from understanding at the time that it could be the same for the babies.

It took me another ten years to discover that there was no age limit to this phenomenon and that a baby of a few hours old could abandon himself to one arm and refuse another, escape from an imposed relationship to cling to an unknown but more secure human being, then slip into his brain and inhabit his thoughts.

2 - Impossible connection, amorphous baby

How to protect yourself from a too powerful spell

In medicine, quarantine and isolation remain proven methods to reduce the risk of contagion. In our technological world of hyper-connection, the easiest way to protect yourself from the attack of a computer virus, between the moment the danger is detected and the day an antiviral response proves effective, is to disconnect. Tales and legends also teach us that in human life falling asleep can be a convenient way to escape from evil spells, or to escape death.

Thus, the Grimm brothers tell us that Snow White survived the evil spell cast by the queen - her stepmother in the final text but her natural mother in the first version of 1812 - by plunging into a deep coma. A whole team of small social workers, with various characters, grumpy, jovial and so many others, had taken care of her during her hospitalization in an intensive care unit - she was installed in a very large transparent incubator - until her love for a young prince finally allowed her to emancipate herself from the deadly maternal hold and to recover the freedom to live.

Another heroine, Sleeping Beauty, was protected from a fate just as bad by a good fairy, probably a great-aunt, who allowed her to disconnect from the harmful waves of the Carabosse and to wait for better days to reconnect to life. A long and difficult treatment. Indeed, she had to spend thirty-six thousand five hundred and seventy-five days in a medical reanimation unit - imagine the bill for the Social Security! -, sheltered in her transparent bubble. An older version of the legend tells that she was almost devoured by her stepmother, an ogress, and was saved once again, *in extremis*, by her prince.

In these tales, the two young girls were protected from a mortifying family climate, either by a fairy or by dwarfs, who acted as substitute parents until the princesses were emancipated.

To be protected and to become capable of freeing itself from toxic influences, which requires quality affective supports, here are the two essential conditions so that a baby can build itself in difficult relational conditions. This can sometimes require a passage by a service of psychic reanimation when the spell has proved too powerful.

Melanie at the maternity ward

Melanie, first day

When she was born, Melanie was full of vitality and tone. A baby in good shape who was responsive to human voices and interested in the faces of the people around her. Nothing to report, everything was reassuring, the light of the world seemed beautiful.

However, the intellectual difficulties of her parents caused some concern to the medical team of the maternity hospital and it was decided even before the birth to keep this mother and baby a few days longer than usual under observation, as a precaution.

Melanie, second day

Melanie began to elaborate her masterpiece, a sensory and relational encyclopedia of the world, an immense work that would occupy her all her life. Melanie began this masterpiece with practical work: the bath.

It is an impressive physical and psychological experience for a newborn to be confronted, from the very first hours of his extra-uterine life, with the radical change in his internal and external environment that represents the fact of going brutally from a state of almost unchanging physiological stability to a state of perpetual imbalance. The bath time, which is far from being a peaceful return to the intra-uterine liquid environment, is a good example.

However, modern pediatric science often sees in this necessary practice of child care only a reason of hygiene, while Plutarch revealed to us, twenty centuries ago, the meaning and the necessity of this ritual ceremony of passage: "For nothing is so imperfect, so destitute, so naked, so shapeless, so so soiled as man when we see him at his birth. He is almost the only one to whom nature has denied even an immaculate access to the light. All smeared with blood and full of dirt, it is more reminiscent of a murder than a birth, it is not good to touch, nor to pick up, nor to cover with kisses, nor to take in the arms, except for those who naturally love it[6]." In ancient times, the first bath was therefore the time when the child was accepted by the *pater familias*, and was recognized as a member of the family well before being given a name and presented to the ancestors. It introduced a separation between what is kept and what is rejected, between the clean and the dirty, between the pure and the impure, between animality and humanity, between barbarism and culture, between the beast that licks with its saliva and the man that purifies with water. An essential and serious rite, although it is associated with the wonderful welcome of a new life. Otherwise, the newborn was abandoned naked, with only the repulsive tags of childbirth for clothing.

---

6. Plutarch, Moral works. Book VI, 32, On the love of offspring.

For Melanie, at this moment, it is only to leave the softness of the elastic and warm contact of an animal body and to find herself on a comfortable but inert and inanimate surface. The limbs that one pulls one by one to undo the small clothes. A wave of coolness progresses on the surface of the skin of the extremities towards the mass of the body. The warm breath of a face that bends. A small current of air that accompanies its movements. The acid and milky smell of the first stools. The scent of a body stirring above. A large hand lifting her back, a thumb slipped under the armpit. The head balanced on a wrist. The time of levitation, the body carried in suspension. Unstable translation before reaching the liquid surface. Then comes the most vivid moment, the contact then the progressive immersion in the water, even if the temperature is perfect. It is an acute sensation that the child will revisit during the experience of his first baths in open water, a lake, a river, the sea, where one plunges into it step by step to tame the liveliness of the sensations that comes from abandoning oneself to the elements, water, sun and wind, while leaving the weight of the earth. Losing your footing. The flood that rises at a crazy speed, faster than the tide that catches you at Mont-Saint-Michel. The sea rises, compresses the belly, weighs on the breathing, then finally stops, spread out, at the level of the shoulders. Saved. A breath and a sigh. On Melanie's skin the invisible liquid transmits its warmth, never exact. Gravity fades, a part of the body floats. The musculature gives up the fight, calms down little by little, the arms spread, the hands open, the fingers loosen, the legs relax, the toes relax. The lungs unfold again. A slight relaxation of the face appears after this concentration of sensations in so few moments.

The first affective supports of the baby: the glance and the word

His gaze that seeks another

When entering the world, the first bath, which does not respond to any physiological need but to archaic anthropological rituals, represents a physical and initiatory ordeal that cannot be crossed without words that guide, reassure, temper, orient, and tell the story of the body and its emerging emotions by giving them meaning. Melanie waits for words that tell her about the new perceptions of the geography of her body, traversed by the elements, the water, the air, the heat and the new gravity. Melanie hopes for a word that tells her her place in the world. You are my child, I am your mother, I am your father, we take and will take great care of you. Plunged into the heart of these sensations and the emotion of this expectation, Melanie seeks to meet a human gaze. Melanie is looking for her mother's gaze.

Absent

A mother absent, or present on the fringe, at the edge - of the bathtub in this case. She gives her daughter a bath but looks at the edge of the tub. Then she looks at her daughter, her arm, her feet, her head, her face but not her eyes. Melanie looks for her mother's eyes, does not find them, drifts and clings to a detail of her clothing. Then her mother stares into her daughter's eyes. But Melanie has moved on. This misunderstanding of looks is replayed several times, without resolution. The mother does not call her voice to make up for this failure. Absent addressee, return to sender, but without notice of passage of the letter carrier. They diverge and do not meet. Like a Feydeau play, when the husband enters the scene on the courtyard side, the lover is exiting on the garden side and vice versa. It's hard to know if the mother is running away from her daughter or if it's Melanie who can't keep up with the mother's timing.

It is true that this mother took care of this baby, but when it pleased her, as if she were a bathing boy who was taken and left, and in a mechanical way. Melanie's cries did not provoke any reaction from her. The whole night and late morning she did not wake up to feed her.

In order to compensate for these deficiencies, the nursery nurses thought of drawing a pictorial schedule with the feeding times. But without success. When she was taking care of Melanie, her gestures were abrupt and inappropriate. She did not support her head or could grab her by one foot. She did not look at her or talk to her. Melanie had no place in her head.

Melanie was alone.

Melanie's loneliness

Melanie, third day

Melanie seeks to continue her genesis of the world but she runs into the very door of loneliness. With no emotional connection available, Melanie encounters only a depopulated world. How, in these conditions, to have the desire to live? In order to begin to think, that is to say, to exist, a baby needs to encounter the thoughts of another human being who cares about him. And to do this, it is an archaic message that it sends, tenuous, delicate to decipher, like the long and overlapping truhuhulhuhut of the first analogical modems at the time of the connection or the very spaced monotonal beep of the first Sputnik.

Melanie is crying, it's time for her bottle. But the mother has started her meal tray. Melanie continues to cry. The mother turns her back to her. The nursery nurse points out Melanie's crying. The mother, disturbed in her meal, growls.

The parents watch television, the baby cries, nothing happens. They don't disconnect from the sound or the image of the television.

Melanie, day four

Melanie is insecure by her mother's unreassuring gestures. She awkwardly lifts Melanie by grabbing both her little shoulders with both hands, her head falling backwards. Then, realizing that she no longer has a free hand to support her neck, she puts her head first on the changing table.

She plunges her into the bath. Melanie, always meets only the emptiness and the absence.

Suddenly, in a final vital burst, Melanie tries everything. Distraught, she is no longer looking for her mother, but turns her gaze towards another human presence. It is the childcare worker of the service, present at this moment at the mother's side. She perceived Melanie's distress and moved forward a little, leaning over the scene. At that moment Melanie clutched her gaze to hers like a drowning man clings to the rope that has been thrown to him and offered to him. This professional supports this glance and does not let it go any more. She never takes her eyes off Melanie. A human has finally agreed to answer this bottle thrown into the sea, the interstellar beep-beep and the bumpy truhuhulhuhut of old modems. Man does not like to imagine himself alone in the universe and in the absence of a God, whom some fear or others doubt, he hopes to discover, or dreads, other lost ones, similar or dissimilar, extraterrestrials by definition.

A little later, the mother was watching television while giving the bottle, without any exchange with her baby. Melanie kept her eyes closed. The nursery nurse turned down the sound, spoke to Melanie who opened her eyes and clung to her gaze again.

Melanie has given up the human trade

But for Melanie, it was already almost too late.

The wandering spell in the sidereal desert was too powerful. Melanie had joined the limbo and given up any possibility of connection in the presence of her parents.

Melanie, fifth and subsequent days

What is the use of counting time when everything is the same? Melanie, passive, now also absent, avoided human contact, both with the staff and with her parents. Her body had softened, her movements rarefied. She hardly moved her small limbs. She no longer opened her eyes, even when she was being fed. She was in a very serious emotional coma.

The dad, however, was concerned and asked with some pertinence, "Is it normal for her to have her eyes closed all the time?" The mother hadn't noticed anything and was sick of the hospital. She wanted to go home with her silent, lifeless toy.

Melanie, day eight

Nadia, the psychologist of the maternity hospital, alarmed by this relational collapse, asked the nursery nurse to try a desperate maneuver: a psychic massage. A last resort to try to resuscitate her, away from the parents invited by Nadia to come and talk in her office during the operation. Sitting near the crib, her face at Melanie's level, the nursery nurse tries to wake her up with soft words. She knows that Melanie keeps her eyes closed to the world, but she also knows that she is not sleeping. "Melanie, Melanie, I look at you and I know you can hear me." Five minutes, ten minutes, fifteen minutes, nothing helps, Melanie doesn't want to come back among the living.

She is not discouraged by this. The mandate of her team gives her duty and confidence, she refuses to believe that the creation of the world stopped on the sixth day and that everything is played out. She refuses to believe that Melanie left the attraction of the earth, where humans lived, to wander in the infinite desolation of space. She does not want to abandon this lost baby. She continues the reanimation beyond a time that would be reasonable. Besides, the reason has nothing to do in this. After twenty long minutes of invitation to life, Melanie finally raises her head from the small mattress, opens her eyes and looks again at the light of the world.

But the following days, before her departure for the nursery, ordered by the prosecutor, she would never open her eyes again in the presence of her parents, not even at bottle-feeding time. However, at certain times the caregivers perceived that despite her closed eyes, Melanie remained attentive to their voices.

In the absence of a stable, good quality emotional connection, Melanie no longer has the appetite for life or the desire to exist.

Is there any hope left?

The princess of limbo

The first few days in the nursery, Melanie was very weak, her neck needed to be held so that her head would not fall off. Sometimes she falls asleep during the feeding, which she starts greedily, but without swallowing. The milk flows from her mouth through the corners of her mouth. She overflows but does not fill up.

It's the middle of summer, it's a warm day, but Melanie's skin marbles at the slightest change in her environment, testifying to the intense emotions that overwhelm her and that she cannot contain. Children and adults alike express their emotions in every possible color of their face: pink with contentment, white as a sheet, pale as death, green with fear or rage, livid with grief, red with shame, even peony or ruby. Babies have not yet mastered the full range and palette of these emotions, and when they are too intense, the colors mix on the surface of their entire body: their skin can suddenly become mottled, with shadows, redness, fleeting blushes and highlights.

Melanie has an exacerbated perception of everything that touches her skin. Even the contact of the bath water, at the right temperature, where she is gently placed, surrounded by words, makes her faint. Her eyes go backwards, she is even more limp than limp. It is necessary to take her out of the bath, to wrap her up, to hold her close, to speak to her gently so that she comes back to life. Her mothering mothers chose to bathe her in light swaddling clothes to reduce the slightest temperature contrasts and spare her the ordeal of being stripped. A premonitory shroud?

Indeed, the psychic death, impavid figure, eviscerating the souls of the interior, annihilating without shame the least emotions, light, strong or subtle, all the emotions, prowls around.

Melanie never shows up, no crying, no eye contact, no sign of impatience when bottle time approaches. Melanie emerges from her lethargy and sleep very infrequently. It is difficult to distinguish between the times when she keeps her eyes closed, when her face is perhaps less set in wax, and the times when she is asleep. The short moments of wakefulness are used to feed her.

The nights are just as quiet, which is very strange for such a young baby. The ritual question asked to young parents is if their baby is finally sleeping through the night. With Melanie no worries, she sleeps like an angel, an angel who has already gone into limbo, or more exactly, she sleeps in a blissful silence. But just as strange, about once a week, Melanie has a very bad night. She cries a lot and has trouble drinking her bottle. Even more amazing is that on these nights, Melanie will stiffen up when held, as if she is fighting back, when she is so limp the rest of the time. For Coline, our experienced pediatrician, it is not the body that suffers.

A scientific observation of a baby's inner chaos

So our nurse, who is gifted with a beautiful scientific mind, marks with a red dot on the calendar these agitated sleeps and looks for the cause. She quickly noticed that this apparent rhythm corresponded to the nights following her parents' visits. Except once. This is incomprehensible. She investigated further and carefully reread the reports of each of the visits, all of which were written with extreme meticulousness.

The study of the detailed account of these encounters makes it possible to understand that the only time Melanie slept afterwards without crying was when her mother left her lying in her deckchair without trying to carry her. It is true that this mother is clumsy with her daughter. She bumps her against her glasses, puts her hair in her face, does not support her head and puts her in unstable balance on the edge of her knees to the point that the staff is obliged to intervene so that she does not fall. She handles her daughter without talking to her, without looking at her, as if she were a small animal or a celluloid doll. Melanie hardly ever opens her eyes during meetings with her parents.

From her sidereal night, from the confines of the universe, Melanie had sent us a confused message of distress. It was captured and recorded with precision and then deciphered with mastery. Finally something to hold on to in the darkness.

We decided to ask the mother not to take her daughter anymore during visits, explaining that it was essential that Melanie be reassured by her. She resigned herself to this and accepted. Thanks to this sacrifice, Melanie regained her calm sleep. She was a limited mother, who could sulk and get angry when she was upset, but who trusted the professionals to whom the judge had entrusted her daughter. Several times a week we informed the parents of Melanie's progress.

An intensive emotional and psychological care service

To hope to see her come back to life, Melanie au Bois Dormant, the princess of limbo, as white as snow, requires intensive emotional and psychic care.

Faced with this lethargy, the whole team of the nursery is mobilized. Each intervention by a mothering staff member is preceded by a word of greeting and a time of waiting before taking her in the arms for example. Melanie is often carried against herself or in a sling, glued to the warmth of a body, gathered in the contact of a skin. In her crib she is cradled very tightly so that she does not feel the emptiness around her. During feedings, her mother puts her face to face so that Melanie does not have to make the effort to turn her head in search of a human gaze, which she would not do. As soon as Melanie opens her eyes, she sings her little songs to get and keep her attention. Already the baths are going better, but Melanie is still wrapped in swaddling clothes before emerging from the water as was Osiris, cut into pieces by the evil Set, but gathered in strips and thus brought back to life by the goddess Isis. The shroud became a bandage and a psychic bandage.

Finally, she opens her eyes, accepts again the meeting of glances as in her very first days. Melanie now turns her head when she perceives a familiar voice and then stares at her mothering staff for a long time. She even smiles timidly, then really smiles, which provokes cheers from the team, but in silence so as not to frighten her.

Coming out of the emotional coma

Melanie is 6 weeks old. The nurse who was supposed to give her her bottle is delayed by another child and she is busy not far from Melanie. Suddenly, she hears a chirping sound from a wren that she can't identify, followed by a small, very discreet cry that gradually grows in volume: Melanie is finally demanding to be taken care of!

Melanie sometimes manifests herself but we must blow on this ember, feed this little flame and take care to answer her calls correctly and each time. This requires a great deal of consistency in her care on the part of her mothering staff, day after day, with constancy, which is not easy to manage with the responsibility of the six little children in this group.

Melanie now opens her eyes to the world around her. She now looks at the spectacle of other children moving, playing, talking, shouting.

At the visit, the mother, who has agreed to stop holding her, remains at a distance, a situation that forces her, because of the physical space that separates them, to observe her daughter and talk to her. She is surprised to meet her eyes and to hear her chattering. She then sees Melanie attempt a few small smiles, very fleeting, almost conventional giggles. But for the first time, this mother expresses a feeling of pride in front of her daughter's expression. The psychic distance has diminished.

But Melanie's desire to exist remains fragile, as soon as a situation makes her uncomfortable she takes refuge in sleep again. And if no one is available to be with her when she emerges from the depths, she immediately falls back into them.

The solution: invest in very high speed internet?

3 - Don't take the limbo princess for a retard

Melanie meets Esther

Because of this persistent lethargy, although she had made significant progress, we decided to place Melanie in the care of a foster family in order to provide her with a very high-speed emotional connection, without the risk of a load break, twenty-four hours a day, seven days a week.

At three and a half months old, Melanie met Esther.

The first approach is complicated. Melanie stares at Esther but she herself expresses only weariness and heaviness, the features of her face fall. The cheeks, the lips, the eyelids, the forehead, everything is flaccid. She nevertheless addresses a timid smile to him.

Esther tells us that when she allowed herself to hold Melanie she felt like a soft baby, like a big doughnut of hot, soft marshmallow that the fairground confectioners enjoy lifting over their cauldron and watching it stretch out under its own weight, inexorably slow. No muscular holding. Her small body rested passively in the offered arms, but whatever was sticking out of them flowed slowly and seemed to want to stretch to the ground. She did not hold her legs, nor her pelvis, nor her back, which she let fall and spread slowly in the void. A baby that was not holding itself and that we had to make sure to pick up all the stretched pieces.

Esther has to wake Melanie up to take her milk, she never asks for it. She has no appetite. Time also goes by forever. It was a real ordeal to get her to drink a simple bottle, rarely finished. She would starve herself without making any demands. Esther noticed that by curling Melanie up in the fetal position, gathering her up against her in this way, which is very uncomfortable with one arm, holding the bottle with her other hand, she sucked better. By the end, Esther is drenched in sweat as she tries her best to keep Melanie awake.

But if Melanie does not show any appetite, she quickly shows herself eager for contact, staring at Esther with great intensity. She also shows her attention to the slightest noises in the environment and to all the movements of the inhabitants of the house. Soon the smiles multiply, addressed to each member of the family.

Melanie always remains passive in her cradle but little by little at the time of the change, fixing Esther of the glance, she smiles to her and starts to chirp. Soon she grabs her feet to suck on her toes. An intense muscular effort - try to do the same! It is by looking at Esther, by addressing her babbling, that she produces her athletic feats.

The baby clings to the gaze that carries him

Now, when Esther wants to pick her up, whereas before Melanie would sink like a soft marshmallow, she lifts her legs like a baby koala and then holds her head firmly on a solid back and stares at Esther with her eyes. It is this gaze directed at Esther, and received five out of five, that transmutes Melanie from an invertebrate thing into a toned little human being. "Good-addressing" or "bad-addressing" is a matter of addressing, a good connection from the sender to a good receiver, and not of training or re-education.

It is necessary to have felt in one's arms the state of limpness or extreme tension of these disconnected and lost babies in order to understand by contrast how from the first days a newborn in good psychological health already makes important physical efforts to adapt and to be in tune with the body which carries it and to become one with it.

When you hold a baby in your arms, he has only his trunk, back, pelvis and the roots of his limbs to cling to you. When you say that a baby is surrendering to your arms, it is really an active attitude on his part that gives you the feeling that he is resting there and the illusion that he is not doing anything for it. A baby carried in your arms or against you is not passive, quite the contrary. It adheres to you by its own weight, it is an intentional gesture on its part.

It is not because a baby is not able to hold his head up for more than a few seconds that he does not know how to relax a little here, while contracting a little there, to become one with the person who supports him, which requires a total physical commitment from him. Of course you hold him, you support him, you hold him, but if he seems so light to you to carry, it is because he holds on to you like a goose to its rock. A baby sticks to you by using its weight and its elastic compactness because it models its musculature to the shapes of your body.

He settles, loves, squeezes, leans, rests, perches, lodges, places himself, anchors himself, nests, blocks himself between the hollows and the bumps, between the firm and the soft of your body to better adhere to it. A comfortable position on your part and assured on his part, that is to say a reciprocal adaptation, frees his arms and legs from parasitic tensions, which allows him to use them to explore with his hand, your mouth, your nose, your eyes, your glasses, your hair, a necklace, earrings while feeling with his foot a knee, a table edge, an armchair, that is to say his very immediate environment His arms, hands, legs and feet are of no use to him to hold on to you, but by their relaxation or stiffness they express his level of security or insecurity. It is enough for him to cry for this tuning to suddenly vanish while tensions appear and make his carrying more complicated. It is the adult who must then make an effort to adapt. "I don't know how to hold him anymore" you say. Attentive parents feel these things intuitively and immediately perceive their baby's level of well-being or discomfort in their arms and adapt to it. It is their baby's memory, a memory of the body before words, which expresses itself without their knowledge. This is why, when faced with certain emotions that surprise us, we do not have the words, because it is our body that remembers and expresses itself. In our defending spirit, archaic emotions sometimes cross us in these very particular circumstances, specific to each one. An old friend told me, astonished to observe these autonomous expressions of his own body, in the anguish that was gripping him when he was faced with his very sick little daughter, in great danger: "At night, tears flow from my eyes and I feel my throat tightening but no words come. I just feel my body crying and my throat tightening."

A psychologically healthy newborn surrenders to loving arms. On the contrary, lost babies, in a situation of affective disconnection, do not know how to put themselves and are either all soft or all stiff, or always in motion but never tuned to the body that carries them. They are as hard as sticks, as elusive as soapsuds, as heavy as sound bags, or they slip away from you like slow worms, always giving the impression that they are going to slip out of your hands and fall away from you because they have not learned to use the roughness of the other person's body in order to land on it and stick to it.

Without a quality emotional bond, no tuning is possible.

Melanie is conducting experiments on the quality and emotional stability of her surroundings

Now Melanie lets her affection for her childminder run wild. She grabs Esther's face with both hands, rubs her nose against hers and goes to snuggle into her neck, wriggling.

In the evening, our big sleeper doesn't want to go to bed anymore. She has noticed that this is the time when Esther is less busy with everyday tasks. She is then bubbly and jargonizes nicely if Esther takes care of it. But as soon as she is put in her crib, she screams, cries and storms. Esther returns. It is all smiles, excitement and great conversations. Esther admires: "She is so funny, she babbles little sentences, very modulated. Esther puts her back to bed and it starts again. Esther, exhausted, ends up lecturing her gently." Melanie is grateful to listen to her and finally falls asleep. But later she wakes up Esther again. When she arrives, Melanie is not crying anymore, on the contrary, she is in great shape. Chipie. Melanie discovers the jubilant power to make Esther's face appear at any time of the day or night, whenever she feels like it. She becomes the creator of the world.

Melanie's defensive strategies

Melanie's lethargy and limpness had been so impressive and so difficult to explain that medical investigations were immediately scheduled in search of an explanatory disease, in parallel with intensive emotional and psychological care. Does she have an intellectual disability? Does she have a brain problem? Is there an illness that slows her awakening? Is it the expression of a genetic anomaly? Several hypotheses had been considered in view of the numbness of her awakening observed during the first weeks. Fortunately, the various specialized consultations did not reveal any disease, but on the contrary allowed us to observe a regular recovery of her development to the point that at 6 months Melanie showed an almost normal development and a reassuring relational appetence, which corresponded to the progress observed day after day.

But the particular circumstances of these appointments at the university hospital were exploited by her father and mother - they were of course associated with them - who took advantage of the opportunity to assert their role as parents by claiming to present Melanie themselves, in their arms, to the consultants. This had a very unexpected effect which reinforced our observations on selective affective connections in babies.

Melanie, 6 months old, is therefore accompanied to a consultation with the neuropediatrician. In the waiting room, the family assistant entrusts Melanie to her father who has requested it. Melanie looks at her father for a while, without smiling, then starts to whine and squirm while turning to Esther. The father gets up and walks to try to calm her down and get her away from this magnet. The maneuver does not work. Melanie suddenly looks really distressed. She then clings to her thumb and starts sucking nervously. This does not soothe her, she rejects her thumb and takes the one on her other hand. She is dissatisfied and cannot reassure herself. The mother who observes the scene then wants to interfere and signals that she will take it. She sits down with Melanie not on her lap but carried fairly upright on her chest in a position as uncomfortable for her as for her daughter. The nursery nurse offers to put her back in a more comfortable position, but the mother refuses. Melanie fell asleep in this oddly balanced position, soon broken by the father who took her back. Melanie has given up, she no longer struggles, she no longer complains. In appearance she has fallen asleep.

Everyone enters the consulting room. The doctor sees a small, fragile baby sleeping soundly in his father's arms. This pediatric brain specialist learns about the circumstances of his birth and his short life. She begins to wonder how she will be able to assess anything about the wakefulness of this baby whose sleep is so heavy. The unusual noises of this foreign place, the unfamiliar voices, the hospitable smells do not disturb her. The mother answers the doctor's questions as best she can. Melanie did not flinch and did not open an eye.

The questions dry up, we will have to move on to the serious stuff, the neurological examination, the infant's reflexes, and the evaluation of his awakening, that is to say, at this age, the quality of the contact and communication. This assumes that the baby is awake and cooperative. This is not an easy task.

The doctor asked the father to give the child to him to put her on the examination table. Melanie, on her back, still asleep, did not flinch. No little moan, no mimicry, not the slightest grin, her face as smooth and inexpressive as ever, her eyes closed. The doctor finally addresses Melanie. She introduced herself, apologized for having to wake her up, and explained that she was going to examine her. Melanie opened her eyes, smiled at her and immediately began to vocalize. The specialist is surprised: "But you don't know me. You woke up and are talking to me! You know you're cute." During the twenty minutes of the examination, which is very long at this age, Melanie remained attentive, available and listening.

Esther and the childcare worker on the ward are amazed at the skills Melanie is showing today in such unusual circumstances as this medical examination, in front of a doctor she does not know. She presents herself as a little girl of her age, with only a slight delay in the process of catching up, and which has nothing to do with what this child had feared when she was only sleeping in her parents' arms, to the point of raising the suspicion of a cerebral malformation or hypothyroidism for example. When her caregiver dressed her, Melanie continued to smile and gesticulate gently as she chatted. When she leaves the hospital, she will not go back to sleep in the car.

The brain specialist sent us this letter: "During the consultation, I was able to observe Melanie's ability to go into a total inhibition, to enter a deep sleep as soon as she was in her parents' arms, whereas as soon as she changes arms she becomes animated and shows normal developmental skills for her age."

At 8 months old, during a consultation with the professor of genetics called to the rescue to evaluate the risk of a disease with an unpronounceable name, Melanie will reproduce the same scene of a blinking sleep depending on who is taking care of her.

The nursery nurse is waiting for the parents in the waiting room with Melanie on her lap. She is awake, chatting and smiling. Her parents arrive. Her father asks to pick up his daughter. In his arms, Melanie quickly shows signs of dissatisfaction, squirms, rubs her eyes and hangs from her thumb. When she entered the consultation room, her mother carried her. Melanie no longer talked or smiled, she whimpered and still clung to her thumb during the interview. When the teacher examines her, Melanie's mood changes, she opens up and becomes available and willing to listen.

When the father took her back while waiting for a blood test, Melanie immediately fell asleep. Her father puts her down on the treatment table and Melanie wakes up immediately when the nurse comes in. The little girl smiles and chats with him. She did not fall back asleep on the trip home.

Melanie the hacker

During parental visits to the nursery, Melanie now accepts some eye contact and short verbal exchanges to which she sometimes responds with a few lallations. But as soon as one of her parents approaches or shows the intention to pick her up, Melanie clings to the professional at her side with her eyes, then becomes agitated and whines if the parent insists. If one of them is too invasive, but still comes to hug her, or if the meeting lasts more than 15 minutes, Melanie closes her eyes or may fall asleep, only to wake up as if by magic at the simple announcement that the visit is over. She immediately regains her energy and vitality in the arms of her caregiver.

Parental visits remain difficult for Melanie. They are unpredictable, depending on her parents' moods. Melanie sits in her deckchair or lies on the floor and agrees to look at them, and sometimes tries to smile at them. One day, her mother got angry, upset about a detail, while she was carrying Melanie, which she always asked for. She forgot that she had a baby in her arms, became agitated, raised her voice, made sudden gestures, and Melanie found herself caught in a storm, with air holes, deafened by thunder, and tossed about unmercifully.

From that day on, Melanie became more suspicious of visitors. When Melanie arrives in the waiting room before the meeting, she is on the alert. She cranes her neck to watch the door where her parents enter as soon as she hears footsteps on the stairs. She has also become very sensitive to any strong words and looks at Esther intently until she has been reassured by a few soothing signals.

To cope with this insecure situation, Melanie found herself forced to exercise defensive hypervigilance and developed amazing strategies. The limbo princess is not a retard. On the contrary, she showed genius in these difficult circumstances.

Melanie is exactly 6 months and 3 weeks old. At the visit, her father, always angry to see his daughter clinging to the gaze of the professional present, whether Melanie knew him or not, tried to isolate her. As in the hospital waiting room, he tried to cut Melanie off from this attraction. But the little princess has grown up. She will no longer fall back into the same malaise that she had shown in the circumstance, when she had striven to suck her thumbs nervously without succeeding in soothing herself.

On this day, with his back deliberately turned to Diane who is framing the meeting, the father holds Melanie quite low against him, her little head against his chest. He uses his own body as a screen and his daughter is prevented from looking over his shoulder at Diane. It is a winter evening and rainy, the shutters of the room are closed. Melanie spots the reflection of Diane's face on the window, which has become a mirror because of the darkness outside. Diane suddenly notices Melanie staring at her through the window. Melanie has discovered the hacking of emotional connections. They exchange glances and files on the sly through this interface[7]. On

---

7. This is obviously not what is called in psycho-logy "the mirror stage" so well described by Henri Wallon and recycled by Jacques Lacan. Diane sees Melanie, Melanie sees Diane but neither of them perceives her own image and even less together on this improvised psyche. Moreover, Melanie does not yet recognize her own image. It is the perceptible image of the other to which she is attached.

reflection, Diane thinks that Melanie must have already been using this ploy for two or three weeks, but that she herself has only noticed it so clearly today. Melanie, like a true screen hacker, has turned the deadly mirror spell of the Snow White tale to her advantage. "Mirror! Mirror!..."

Melanie's story is typical of the phenomenon of babies' selective affective connections, of this innate capacity that they have to know how to protect themselves from inappropriate interactions, on the one hand, and of this competence to seek out quality affective support with relevance, on the other. Adults must be available and sensitive to the tenuous signals that a baby sends out, and they must agree to respond to them and make a reasoned choice to occupy this uncomfortable position.

Princess Melanie grants audience

It is the day of the retirement party of our head of department. An intense moment where so many shared memories resurface, some light, some hard, but all rich in the magic of work well done, where the only reference standard was the good of the child and the only objective was the coherence of the team work. A moving moment.

Esther came with Melanie who will soon be 9 months old. There are many people and excitement around them. Melanie stays safely in the arms of her childminder.

Now that Melanie has learned to stand against Esther, to lean on Esther, she knows how to occupy this position, as if it were a stronghold, won by hard struggle, and that she finally reigned there. From this secured dungeon, the hand put on Esther's arm, gesture at the same time of possession and reassurance - three small fingers tighten by safety the fabric of the sleeve -, she then looks at you, measures you, examines you. But before she gives you a smile, which is not instantaneous, you have to introduce yourself with humility, state your identity, your function, explain why you are interested in her, the meaning of your approach, and then, as a good princess, Melanie will grant you audience. Short. She knows her place in the world. Precious.

She gave me this grace.

This example, and those that will follow, reveal to us an observable and universal but still unknown reality: from the very first moments of its extra-uterine life, the baby scans its environment in search of the person who is the most secure for it. The baby has an internal affective radar and connects to the best psychic terminal at his disposal, that is to say to the person - adult or child - who is the most available to answer his needs and to metabolize his emotions, without worrying about the meanders of filiation or biological reality. They orient their emotional choices according to the quality of the answers they receive, without waiting to learn how to read a family record book. He goes by feeling, as fast and as short as possible.

This is a confusing conclusion, hard to believe, I agree. It goes against everything that is said about babies - that a child can only depend on its mother or that an infant is only a vegetative being - but it becomes obvious as soon as we accept to open our eyes. If a mother is psychically available to respond to the messages emitted by her newborn, the latter will of course turn to her. But if she is not available for him, the baby will make other choices or let himself die.

The baby is deprived of psychic apparatus and must for its safety and its own conservation be lodged in an available brain like a small marsupial. It is a question of life or death, of physical and psychic survival. It uses your intelligence of the world the time to learn to manage alone. It's a temporary brain rental. Good availability required, broadband connection essential.

4 - FIONA, ONE MONTH AND A HALF

Baby hacked your brain

If a baby's physiological autonomy is already not very long, two, three, four hours maximum between pit stops, its psychological autonomy is much weaker. He doesn't need your concrete presence all the time, but you must be able to answer him at any time. You sit on the jump seat in the anteroom waiting for him. There is no such thing as a part-time parent. Baby needs to experience the excellence and effectiveness of the care of those around him. He is testing your availability to show up and meet his every need, no matter what the circumstances. You are on the alert and you think about him very often. You react even before he needs it. "Hush! I thought I heard him whine in his sleep. Do you think I need to go check on him?" Even after weeks of choppy nights, exhausted by erratic feeding schedules, you pull your periscope out of the abyss of a sleep that had reached the depth of a general anesthetic before your baby even clamored. When baby finally sleeps through the night, you still wake up at the usual time of his call while he sleeps the sleep of the blessed. Because he knows you're there. He has parasitized you, he is fine with it and that is what saves him from everything.

You don't have to make any effort to reach that almost sickly state that Winnicott called "primary maternal preoccupation". Baby has done it for you. He has taken up residence in your brain and you can no longer dislodge him. He is the one who has connected and it has become impossible for you to forget him. For baby it is an extraordinary guarantee of security. He doesn't have to worry about anything anymore, you do it for him. He has discovered the facilities and advantages of outsourcing: all the benefits, without any risk. He is no longer on alert, you are on alert for him.

Fiona, so young, already discouraged by the trade of her fellow men

Fiona was not so lucky when she started her life. Her mother, a young schizophrenic woman who had broken away from care, had refused from the beginning of her pregnancy to resume contact with the hospital team that had previously followed her and was opposed to any therapeutic or medicinal treatment. Since then, the young woman's psychological state had deteriorated considerably and her adaptation to reality had become uncertain.

This mother's early relationship with her baby was very chaotic. She had certainly shown a real interest in her child but she could also disconnect very quickly when she was in the grip of unexpected and sudden preoccupations which made her completely unavailable for her daughter. The maternity ward, concerned about this maternal attention with variable geometry, according to the capricious evolutions of her psychological state, had kept her more than ten days in observation before letting her go back to a mother-child reception structure. She had been advised to read about how to take care of a baby. This was a laudable but naive intention, as the know-how to meet a baby's needs cannot be learned from books. Winnicott wrote[8]: "A mother must draw her knowledge from deep within herself, without necessarily using the form of intelligence that uses words. Most of what a mother does with her baby is not through words. This is obvious, although we tend to forget it." The richness of the encounter and the quality of the emotional relationship with a baby depend much more on a disposition of the mind than on knowledge. They call upon experiences and emotions so primitive that our conscious memory, based on images and words, has kept no trace of them.

Fiona's mother was therefore an eclipsing mother who could turn away from her daughter at any moment if the professionals at the facility did not help her get back on the same orbit as her baby.

Sometimes she had an impulse to call her neighbor and leave Fiona in her care to go live her life. At these times, she no longer cared about her baby. As a result, Fiona was severely destabilized by the increasing disorganization of her daily care. She cried a lot, lost weight, her eyes darkened and she was overcome with extreme fatigue.

Faced with certain sentimental complications, the mother decided overnight to leave the reception center with Fiona, without a clear and reassuring destination. This decision proved to be worrying because of the absence of any anticipation of the baby's needs. The mother, exalted and logorrheic, carried away by her feelings of love, refused to listen to reason about the attention and consideration to be given to the care of such a young child. "She will follow me everywhere, I am her mother."

This is what alerted the social workers. A baby cannot be left in a situation as unpredictable as it is risky, the prosecutor, seized in urgency of this situation of imminent danger, ordered the immediate placement of Fiona in the nursery.

Fiona was then only 6 weeks old.

---

8. WINNICOTT (Donald W.), *Le Bébé et sa mère*, Paris, Payot & Rivages, coll. "Science de l'homme", 1992, *loc. cit.* p. 92.

4 - Fiona, one month and a half

Fiona arrives at Monique's house

Diane, the nursery nurse on the ward, was able to talk to the mother in the presence of her baby. The mother had agreed to entrust Fiona with personal objects, in particular her baby carriage, so that she would not feel too lost.

Diane accompanied Fiona to the home of Monique, a nursery assistant on the ward. Fiona was a very small flea who seemed very fragile, very sick and very insecure. Fiona was very tired. She took her first bottle in Monique's arms. Monique then put her to bed in her baby carriage, which she knew, but in a room that she did not know. Fiona cried, fussed, got upset and seemed very distressed in this new place and being entrusted to unknown people. At that moment, Fiona had no way of understanding the difference between these new arrangements, which were intended to provide her with greater stability, and the impromptu and erratic care that her mother was used to.

Fiona did not calm down. Monique took her back in her arms. Fiona did not succeed in reassuring herself there. She held on very stiffly and then turned and twisted. She was inconsolable.

Then Diane speaks to her. Fiona, between two sobs, hears her voice, turns her head, looks at her and then listens:

"Fiona, you are here with Monique who will take care of you. Sometimes you were afraid with mom, who was too sick to take care of a baby and didn't know how to support you, and carry you, and comfort you. You were certainly also afraid to fall out of her arms. But now Monique is holding you well, you won't fall. And Monique, while you are at her house, will always be there for you. She won't disappear. You can trust her, she will stay close to you.

You also worry about mom, about who will take care of her. She won't be alone, there will be grown-ups to help her. And your mom needs to get better.

You can sleep in peace here at Monique's house. Next week, you will see your mother again. I hope she gets better."

Monique hears Diane talking and feels Fiona against her as she slowly relaxes. It's as if Diane's words were slowly permeating Fiona's entire interior. She loves herself against Monique, her body softens. She ends up putting her head in her neck. Again, for a brief moment, she struggles, a sob, but Diane speaks to her again and she falls asleep.

Monique can't believe how quickly Fiona felt reassured when she heard Diane talk to her, even though she knows so little about her.

Difficult to relearn human contact

Nevertheless, with Monique the beginnings were difficult.

As soon as she wakes up, Fiona avoids Monique's gaze, proof if it were needed that a baby who loses confidence in his parent can also quickly come to distrust other humans.

The following days, instead of looking for Monique's eyes, Fiona stares at a vague spot on the ceiling or lets her gaze wander to the side. Fiona is hypervigilant, on the alert, worried at the slightest noise and scans without respite everything that happens around her. Her sleep is very fragile, she wakes up at the slightest creak or when she perceives an unknown voice. Her face is often crossed by a worried expression, she then tightens her eyelids and contracts the tuft of her chin. But she doesn't cry, which is what an "ordinary" baby would do in this situation. She gives the impression of being very attentive to her environment while trying to make herself forget. She can spend very long moments looking passively and expressionlessly at the void around her.

When Monique picks her up, carefully and with gentle words, Fiona is like a piece of wood. Instead of putting her head on Monique's shoulder she arches her back and throws her head back.

Fiona avoids the gaze of humans and shuns physical contact. Six weeks were enough to discourage her from trading with her fellow humans.

But in four days the situation will change completely.

During these four days this little flea will suddenly gain 10% of her weight[9] . Then little by little she starts to trust Monique. She now accepts to meet her eyes, which does not prevent her from staring at the ceiling at other times. During the feeding, she relaxes and can grasp an offered finger. When everything is calm, she manages to let herself go and abandon herself in the arms of her childminder.

When she wakes up, everything has to start over. Fiona rolls her eyes back and Monique has to talk to her gently before she comes back online. She remains on the lookout, anxious about everything. Monique has found that putting her in a little bouncer in a place where she can observe the environment and not be surprised by events she can't watch any more reassures her. However, she still shows a lot of tension at the slightest novelty. All this testifies to the agitated life that had been hers until then: a chaotic daily life, without any security, and the lack of psychic availability of her mother who did not always have the head to think about her daughter.

In the following days, Fiona gradually calms down, accepts better the look, smiles, chats. Now she suddenly becomes animated when she sees Monique appear in her field of vision. She eats well and continues to gain weight.

---

9. The usual beliefs of the public, but also of the vast majority of childcare professionals, about the negative effects of an early separation of a baby from parents who are not suited to take care of him or her are tenacious. They generally prejudge the impossibility for a baby to survive without his mother and his great suffering if he were to be separated from her. However, when the proposed affective environment is of quality, in a nursery or in a foster family, the babies benefit from their placement. In our nursery, the most striking proof of this beneficial effect is that if half of the babies are admitted with a delay in their weight and height, we observe for half of them a rapid resumption of their growth. This is simply due to an improvement in their emotional and psychological conditions.

Fiona panics when she finds her mother

The mother was authorized by the judge to come and see Fiona.

First visit

During this meeting, the little girl, who was getting better and better, showed great anxiety, a very strong defensive vigilance and an intense search for reassurance with the professionals who accompanied the visit: Diane, who welcomed her, and Lucile, our psychologist, whom she met for the first time.

The mother throws herself on Fiona without giving her time to recognize her. She forgets to speak to her, to say hello. Lucile tries to curb this outburst and invites her to wait, to start by greeting her baby. But she rushes in and pulls Fiona out of the nursery nurse's arms, not without some rudeness because of her haste.

Fiona stiffens in her arms and her head goes backwards. Her whole body is tense like a bow, toes included. Her mother tries to give her a kiss, Fiona flinches, closes her eyes and twists again, turning her head.

Fiona panics, her eyes sweep over bright spots, window, ceiling, deliberately turning her head to escape her mom's gaze. Forced to look, she stares not at her mother's eyes but at the margin of her hair. Soon Fiona can hear that Diane and Lucile are still present in the room. From then on, she will not stop trying to catch their gaze or to turn towards their voices, which makes her feel more secure. This affective disarray between Fiona and her mother is also manifested by the disadjusted attitudes of the bodies. Fiona imperceptibly slips from her mother's arms. It becomes necessary to help her to put Fiona back at ease.

To try to nourish this time of meeting, the hour of the visit was fixed on the time of the feeding-bottle. It is proposed to the mother to make her drink to Fiona. But there also the baby does not manage to find its place in the arms of its mother. They have to readjust several times without finding the good tuning. But it is too late and Fiona does not want to finish her bottle. Then the mother does not manage to make her burp. Diane takes Fiona back and she quietly finishes her milk in her arms.

The mother takes her back on her knees. She makes great declarations of love to her of a disaffected voice: "I love you, you are my flesh, you are my blood, you are my being", but Fiona almost slips on the ground. In spite of advice given with delicacy, the mother, clumsy, has gestures supported, almost brusque towards Fiona to try to take again it in her arms.

Diane took Fiona back into her arms. In this way, she is able to give her mother smiles, glances and hugs. A certain physical distance from her mother is more reassuring for Fiona than too much physical proximity. Once in Diane's arms, she is able to communicate with her mother. This is a strange phenomenon that we observe very often with certain parents who are very confusing for their baby. From far away it's ok, too close, hello the damage!

Like Melanie, Fiona, during this visit, seeks to distance herself from her mother and find security with people who are almost strangers to her. Fiona was only 7 weeks old at the time.

The observations of these visits, the attitudes of the mother, the reactions of Fiona, left us wondering about the seriousness of the chaos in which this baby had lived during six long weeks with her mother. And how much Fiona remembered it, still suffered from it and was apprehensive about finding her mother. Such situations are imperative and absolute child psychiatric emergencies, but how many professional teams are trained in these observations? Too few, too rare!

This visit caused a lasting psychic disorganization in Fiona. After this meeting, the behavior of this very young baby became very worrying again and the progress made by Monique disappeared for several days before Fiona started to move forward again. The following encounters had the same consequences and Fiona's malaise worsened from visit to visit.

Diane was amazed:

"Fiona was fine at Monique's house last week. After the visit, it was the opposite. I found a translucent Fiona, without any thickness, indifferent. She even arches her back when Monique gives her a bath and she doesn't look at us anymore. If I hadn't known her before, I would have thought she was a handicapped little girl, stiff like a quadriplegic child.

A layperson amazed to observe a baby's emotional discrimination

Second parent meeting

Fiona arrives calm and relaxed in Diane's arms. She has an open mind about the world. Their path crosses that of the new head of the administrative department who, no doubt not too comfortable in the midst of this army of nursery nurses and very small children, often declares that he understands nothing about babies. But he is a polite and civil man, probably much more competent than he announces. Politeness and civility are essential qualities to communicate with babies. Babies are dependent, but we are obligated to them.

He doesn't know Fiona, and Fiona doesn't know who this man is. He passes her, he greets her. Fiona is only a baby but there is no reason to ignore her under the supposed pretext of an inferior condition inherent to her very young age. He speaks to her gently. Fiona answers him with a smile and tries to communicate. She addresses to him a sustained glance decorated with some small mimics. It's so funny to see the effort Fiona makes to capture the attention of another human and the attraction she manages to exert on this one, who claims to know nothing about babies. Communicating with a baby requires only that you be available to him, and that you let him take the initiative in his connection strategy. It is he who makes you a subject, a subject of interest, a subject of curiosity, a subject of conversation, a subject of request, a subject of affection and attachment, a subject at all.

Our head of department, this polite man, suddenly notices that Fiona withdraws on herself and closes her eyes. She squirms, settles down, seems very uncomfortable. He doesn't understand, is surprised, and opens up to Diane when the mother appears close to them. Fiona had seen and recognized at distance her mother and already apprehended her contact.

Our department head would later come back and tell us how surprised he was to see such behavior in such a young baby. He couldn't believe it. This department head is making progress.

That day the mother is invaded by interior preoccupations which she tells in a bad way by speaking quickly and much, going from one thing to the other without link between them, jumping from one thing to another. She delivers what comes to her mind without restraint or modesty. It is difficult to follow the thread of her speech and impossible to stem her flow. Her thoughts are running at full speed, mixing her personal relationship worries, the actuality of this visit and her pride in finding her daughter. She speaks to whoever is there, without making any difference between the interlocutors. It is difficult to grasp what she wants to say and who she is trying to address. She is unable to listen to the professionals who try to talk to her. It is impossible to ask her to refocus on Fiona. She is inaccessible.

Diane puts Fiona in the baby carriage hoping that the distance will make contact easier.

But for Fiona everything goes wrong. Fiona is writhing in her baby carriage and refuses eye contact with her mother.

In these conditions the visit turns short.

Family Council

Third parent meeting

The mother's psychological state is more stable today. She asks pertinent questions about her daughter. She speaks to her with a lot of affection and her words are no longer the empty and plated formulas of the first visit or the uninterrupted flow of the second. However, Fiona will immediately show signs of great discomfort at her contact.

Fiona recognizes his voice and turns her gaze to her mother. She holds on to it, but for less than a minute, and does not smile at it. On the contrary, she gets agitated. Her mother takes her to give her her bottle, she calls her gently, she speaks to her. Fiona responds to this dialogue and looks at her mother, but immediately looks away. Fiona has certainly perceived her mother's anxieties, anxieties about the decisions to be made for Fiona's future, which the mother will express a little later during the visit. Then again Fiona arches her back, her head goes backwards and she is no longer in communication with her mother. She closes her eyelids little by little and seems to want to fall asleep, indifferent or even opposed to the various verbal requests of her mother. The mother insists but Fiona does not finish her bottle. She squirms and starts to cry. Between two sobs she seeks the gaze of Diane who accompanies the visit. The mother puts the bottle back into Fiona's mouth and she gags. The mother does not manage to calm her down.

Diane takes it back, Fiona relaxes.

Diane entrusts Fiona again to her mother, who receives her on her lap. Fiona avoids her mother's gaze and looks for Diane's, then becomes agitated and holds her eyes half closed. Put in her baby carriage, she falls asleep immediately. Diane decides to put her to sleep in the adjoining room. Fiona, now at a distance from her mother, wakes up immediately.

Today Fiona also has to meet her maternal grandmother.

Her grandmother announces herself to Fiona, who becomes a little agitated when she recognizes her voice. She stares at her several times in a sweeping motion, not focusing on any particular point, like your office scanner would for a document to be scanned. She finally catches her grandmother's eyes and smiles.

Her grandmother takes her in her arms gently, speaks to her with calm and measure but Fiona still flees from her eyes. It is still too new and too fast for her. Her grandmother is patient and reassures her. Fiona abandons herself and gives her a frank and free smile. Now relaxed she starts, from this perch, to look at what is happening around her.

Her grandmother tells us that her whole family has shown solidarity in order to allow Fiona to be welcomed at her home until her mother gets better. We perceive her lucidity on the seriousness of the psychological state of her daughter but also a lot of respect and attention.

Fiona's mother breaks down, cries and protests. This seems paradoxical because in reality, it is she who had imagined this solution, who had spoken about it and had anticipated this decision. But at the moment of her more official announcement she is caught up in her emotions, and this is fortunate. This shows how precious Fiona is to her even though she has difficulty expressing it in practice. Her mother finds the right words to soothe her, explaining to her the involvement of her brothers and sisters in this family project which was also hers.

The judge approved the project of entrusting Fiona to her grandmother and suspended the exercise of maternal visits on the express condition that the mother resume care and that her psychological state stabilize.

The sacrifice of a mother

This mother, admittedly very ill, had kept, despite appearances, a certain awareness of her psychological problems and tried to do the best for her daughter. Before the birth she had approached the social service. After the birth she agreed to stay in the mother-child reception center. When she was better, she listened to the advice not to rush and to try to reassure Fiona. She had accepted that Diane could intervene to help her settle back in with her daughter in her arms without feeling persecuted. She had also been able to ask for advice during the changeover when she was unsure of herself. Before this last meeting, she had even questioned the future and suggested that Fiona be entrusted to her own mother if it appeared that she herself could not take care of her properly.

I am always moved when I hear struggling parents state their choice to accept being deprived of their child by considering their child's well-being as superior to their own. And they are not rare. These parents, who have not mistreated their baby, but who for various reasons are psychologically incapable of ensuring his education, show by this self-sacrifice a courage that should make many other parents think well of themselves by despising the one-eyed and the crippled.

I am thinking in particular of all those couples who fight over their child like ragamuffins during a separation. Most often noisily, but sometimes also more slyly and in a hidden way, with a bitter edge, without a word higher than the other. The hell disguised by a paradisiacal decor, poison distilled drop by drop and presented as a wonderful elixir: "But you have everything, the computer, the TV, the winter sports, the vacations in Marrakech, what are you complaining about! Stop sulking! It's not because I don't agree at all with your education with the 'other', you know who I mean, that you have to make a big deal of it. Here you go! In fact, you're going to tell him that..."

It is even worse when it is the daily life together, with parents who nourish a hateful relationship towards each other, which can go unnoticed when one is subjected to the diktat of the other and everything seems smooth.

These people do not believe they are pathological parents, but they are certainly hindering the development and growth of their child.

The Foucault pendulum

Fiona was therefore entrusted to her maternal grandmother.

I saw Fiona again when she was 7 months old with her grandmother, who gave me a charming picture of her, a delightful little girl, very communicative, very much in control of her relationship with the adult. Her grandmother was sitting cross-legged on the play mat, one leg unfolded. Fiona posed in confidence on this improvised armchair covered with the dark fabric of a long skirt. Installed well right on the folded calf of her grandmother and occupying this seat with authority, she scanned me with a questioning air. She had put her two hands on the armrests that formed the legs which embraced her and followed our conversation of an authorized ear. Thus secured, she was enthroned and informed.

Fiona had not yet seen her mother for a visit, as her psychiatrist thought it was still premature. But her grandmother was communicating regularly with her mother by webcam. So Fiona regularly heard her mother's voice and she had news and pictures of her daughter.

Fiona had developed and adapted well at her grandmother's house. She regularly went to her nanny's house when her grandmother was working. I noticed the persistent vigilance in her eyes, which betrayed the after-effects of her former defensive surveillance present at the very beginning of her reception in the nursery. But Diane confirmed to me that Fiona had excellent inner security and could leave her grandmother with confidence. The experimental game that Fiona invented and that I had the chance to observe went in this direction and reassured me on this point.

The conversation continued. Fiona slipped onto the carpet and found herself lying on her back. She watched her grandmother talk from below, in a low angle. It was a strategic position that allowed her to keep in touch with her grandmother and the other speakers, Diane and me. Fiona had somehow positioned herself in the center of the device. Her grandmother was amused by her cleverness, smiled at her, and said something to her as she leaned over her. She wore a long pendant which, released by the forward momentum of her torso, then swung at the end of its large chain just above and within reach of Fiona. I was, I must confess, distracted by the scene and anticipated the usual reaction of a baby in such circumstances: to seize the object, to cling to it firmly and to pull very hard. Beware of hair, scrunchies and earrings. It's as appealing to a baby as a Mickey's tail on the merry-go-round for those old enough to ride.

And surprise, which proved to me the psychic and developmental maturity that Fiona had acquired - she was then only 7 months old -, she did not catch it but observed its swing. Then, either with her index finger or by gripping it with her thumb, with precision and delicacy, she practiced pushing it back so that it resumed its oscillating move-ment. This reminded me of the pendulum that Foucault installed in the Pantheon in 1851 to make the reality of the earth's rotation perceptible to the Parisian public. In 1955 this inspired Queen Juliana of the Netherlands to donate a similar pendulum to the United Nations, which is still on display in the lobby of the UN headquarters in New York. On its gold surface she also had the following maxim engraved: "It is a privilege to live today and tomorrow."

Fiona didn't know anything about the rotation of the earth, but at 7 months old she had acquired this inner confidence in the fact that a person, that was her privilege, was available at any moment. She was there yesterday, she is there today and she will be there tomorrow, sometimes moving away, but always coming back, with a regularity of metronome.

4 - Fiona, one month and a half

Better still, Fiona has learned to come to terms with the possible and temporary absence of this person by taming this solitude, by making it her own. When the person moves away and disappears, she is the one who pushed him away with a flick of her wrist; when he comes back, she is the one who made him reappear by the enchantment of her desire; when this person remains, it is she who keeps it, between the thumb and the index finger, as the lover believes to retain near him the loved one by some artifice; and when this person is not there, she remembers it and makes it present by the intermediary of an object which could have belonged to her or that she received as a gift. The game she invents with her grandmother's pendant is for her a representation of all these situations of which she is no longer the helpless and lonely puppet, but of which she imagines she is now the master and the arbiter of the relationship. In this game, because it is one, like the theater or the puppet show, it is no longer she who is the abandoned puppet, because it is she who dismisses and it is still she who invites to come back.

When a baby plays, his parents and educators tenderly consider his activity as physical experiences, new learning or new motor skills. But in reality his games are also authentic psychic stagings that allow him to tame the world and the strangeness of the life of grown-ups who come and go, appear and disappear, and who do not always understand well, or even completely wrongly, the problem of being a baby: wanting a lot and not being able to do anything alone. It seems that grown-ups don't remember very well what it was like to be a baby. So baby invents his own games, thanks to which he develops a very singular logic to make sense of the inexplicable and learns to bear the imperfection that surrounds him. He then proves to be much more intelligent than adults and toy manufacturers because he diverts to his personal use what is formatted for the use of the majority.

Fiona had experienced chaos during her first six weeks of life due to her mother's random responses to her needs. The discontinuous attention of her mother, whose psychic availability to a baby was very variable, had given her no confidence in the stability and solidity of the world. There was no assurance that her hunger would be followed by satiety, that her thirst would be quenched, that being held in her arms was safe, that her cries would be comforted, that someone would see to it that she was neither too hot nor too cold, that an attentive presence would be present when she woke up, that being bathed was a pleasure and not a danger.

I thought it was quite extraordinary that Fiona had managed to regain such confidence in herself and in people, with Monique and then with her grandmother, and in such a short time.

Fiona, a little lost and suffering thing, had become the creator of the world she now organized as she pleased.

5 - Violette, ten days of life

The prodigious memory of Salvador Dalí

On September 30, 1961 Salvador Dalí spoke in front of a camera, but this report was never broadcast. He wore a shiny black silk robe, the sleeves and collar in matte velvet. He recounted, collected and concentrated, the memories of his meeting with Freud in London, more than twenty years earlier. This visit to the master had been arranged on July 19, 1938, by Stefan Zweig, a mutual friend, a little more than a year before the death of the brilliant inventor of psychoanalysis.

With his unique talent for rolling up the *r's* in the most sophisticated way, in a quasi-monastic setting lit by tapered candles, Salvador Dalí, seemed to want to transmit the exact content of their conversation. The interview begins in the very serious tone of a historical documentary. For once, Salvador is more didactic and sober in his speech than Dalí.

But Salvador is still Dalí and this staging lets us see through what it really is: a brilliant artistic mystification. Indeed, what is he talking about? About Freud? No! Or only two words to affirm that the master would have confirmed the validity of his theories. The rest is just an elucubration like Dalí, truculent, magnificent... surrealist. The story of his life in his mother's womb.

What's up? What was Salvador playing in the uterine pool?

Let's hear it:

"Oh yes, I have very clear memories of that. Probably Freud told me that it must correspond to the last two months before birth. But besides, there are characters in history like Casanova, in his Memoirs, he also claims to remember the intra-uterine life. I saw; I saw especially eggs on the 'white place' and then the white of the egg was phosphorescent and it contracted, it moved a little like the mollle watches. The soft watches, the soft side comes from this kind of intra-uterine parrradis in which one is immersed in a kind of viscous and soft environment and in which one feels completely protected from the external world. It's a kind of nirrrvana, a kind of sublime paradise, in the dark, in the heat, and in which one has only the visions provoked probably by the position of the fists on the orbits [he makes the gesture]. Because when you press very hard [he presses his eyes with his fingers] on the orbits, you see what is scientifically called phosphenes. The little children, I remember when we used to play to press the orbits with our fingers to the point of pain to see angels appear, we used to say. These colored circles, the phosphenes, were called angels, which alluded to the intrauterine life. Otto Rank, in his *Trauma of Birth,* shows that when one passes from this absolutely parrradisiac environment to the external world where there is too much light, where everything is too hard, that is why children cry. And moreover it is accompanied at birth very often by a real trauuumatism with symptoms of asphyxia. It is the myth, which is formed at this moment, of the lost paradise. We are chased away from the maternal paradise and that's why most of the suicides want to find again by committing suicide... want to find again this lost paradise [that] we find again in a partial way by recoiling (*sic*) in the sleep, and that's why very often when we approach, after the tiredness, a very restorative sleep and that almost we drool of satisfaction because we approach the sleep, very often there is a frightening thing. We fall into the void [he mimes with his arms the gesture of falling and behind him the credence table and the candles it supports shake] and we wake up with a start and that, precisely, it is a rrrraaaappeal to the trauma of birth, to this idea of falling into the void..."

Yes, without laughing or losing his seriousness, this master of surrealism tells us with great conviction the games that occupied him in the womb. Dalí is going to compare himself to Casanova, who would have affirmed to remember his stay inside the maternal matrix, without blinking.

However, Casanova assures us of the contrary in the preface to his Memoirs: "My story begins with the earliest fact that my memory can provide, it begins at the age of eight years and four months. Before that time, if it is true that *vivere cogitare est*, I was not living, I was vegetating."

Is the maternal womb, as Dalí claims, an extraordinary but lost paradise? And how does this passage influence in one way or another our life on earth? Are we determined by the conjunction of the stars, by the desire of our parents or by possible sudden events during pregnancy and childbirth?

Questions as old as humanity.

The lost paradise of the womb is not always a paradise

Violette comes to us from the maternity ward by order of the prosecutor.

At the service meeting, Bénédicte, her educator, describes Violette's first days at the nursery:

"She did not have a fresh, relaxed face like a ten-day-old baby should have. A bar marked her forehead, she kept her eyebrows furrowed, her complexion pale and her face hollow. Her look remained serious. She looked like a sad little old woman, already wrinkled and withered, who had been blackened throughout an existence of suffering. So young! 10 days old! And already very marked by life.

When she drank, the simple sound of the air sucking through the teat made her jump. She would then contract her face, which she kept tensed for a long time. She would scare herself just by sucking. She would take her bottle with clenched fists. I had never seen that in a baby.

However, we noticed that she liked to be carried, to curl up and to be gathered against us. She felt good in our arms. We felt that she was relaxing there. So we tried to carry her in a sling against us as often as possible. When we carried her like this we also noticed that at the slightest noise, even a discreet one, a simple touch of a child's hand on the table, she was seized with a start followed by a lasting tension of her whole body. It would then take her a while to relax. In these moments, she would also close her face. We would put our hand on her back, on her head, like when a baby is twitching in his mother's breast and she reassures him with her hand on his belly. We were talking to him.

How could a baby so young be so stressed?"

A hellish pregnancy

Our hospital colleagues, who had conveyed to the prosecutor their concerns about the ability of Violette's parents to care for her, had also given us some information about Violette's troubled pregnancy and her mother's troubled personality.

This young mother came from a family of twelve children, like Hugo, Zola and Dickens at the same time. She was a victim of various forms of abuse, rape, violence and serious neglect. She was finally separated at the age of 6 from this mortifying family environment, but far too late to emerge unscathed from so much infamy. She was a child whose psyche was fragile and whose behavior was seriously altered. She was like a skinned child, hyperreactive, impulsive and violent. Her adolescence was explosive, she ran away, abused herself, scarified her skin and made numerous suicide attempts, not being able to bear frustration or disappointment. Paradoxically, she played the role of a bully by persecuting other young people in the various institutions where she was taken in. Children who have only known emotional insecurity and lack of protection sometimes come to lay down the law around them, deluding themselves about the possibility of controlling their environment in this way in order to protect themselves from the hazards of life. Tyrannizing others was an illusory way to avoid surprises and disappointments - serving oneself, putting others at one's service. But when these maneuvers failed, the difficulty of adapting to the world overwhelmed her, and she fell apart. So she attacked herself.

She was hospitalized in a psychiatric environment on several occasions over long periods of time, including two years in a row before she came of age.

It was there that she met her companion who became Violette's father. They ran away together. She did not see the hospital as a protective asylum or as a refuge from illness. On the contrary, she imagined that her freedom was alienated there, and she feared being contaminated by the madness of others. To run away was to escape from the cracks and monstrosity of her childhood life. But it was only running away.

For several months, they led a life of wandering, left to the hazards of the street.

Like many of these young adults with a shattered childhood, the idea crossed her mind that having a child would erase the past and open up a new future.

But she was wearing a contraceptive implant under her skin, opposite her biceps, which had been placed in the hospital. Keeping it was *no baby*. So, with her teeth, she tore off her arm and extracted the implant like some science fiction heroes get rid of the electronic chip that enslaves them.

Pregnant.

She went to tell her mother.

After so many misfortunes with this woman, she still hoped that she would finally pay attention to her. She imagined that this new life would arouse her mother's interest and pride, if not in her, at least in the promise of a child. She said that her mother had suddenly become interested in two of her older sisters when they had a child. So why not her. But all she got was indifference and rejection. "What do you think? You'll be incapable of being a mother!"

A child abuse expert's wise words. Nothing had changed.

This new disenchantment will precipitate her in an unheard-of violence equal to the cruelty undergone in her childhood. She had tried to forget and erase it but her mother, true to herself, had thrown venom and contempt in her face. This young woman was again invaded by hatred and violence that began to overwhelm everything, herself, her companion of misfortune and the whole world.

She had a violent physical altercation with Violette's soon-to-be father. Because of her multiple bruises and her pregnant state, she was put in the maternity ward for observation. She attempted to commit suicide with medication and was transferred to the intensive care unit. Her will to die remaining intact, she found herself interned by order of the authorities, placed in an isolation room and tied up to prevent her from hurting herself. Determined to end it all, she managed to strangle herself with her pajamas despite being heavily sedated and restrained. Back to the intensive care unit.

The psychiatric service proposed a lifting of her hospitalization under constraint since this provision had not solved anything, quite the contrary. Four months pregnant, she went back to wandering with her companion, from city to city, from squat to shelter. She did not worry about the medical follow-up of her pregnancy until, molested in her own family and beaten in her companion's family, she was brought to the maternity ward by the firemen who had found her wandering and pregnant to the neck. She gave birth to Violette as soon as she was admitted.

This appalling story allowed us to explain Violette's stress. She had not known the serenity of a paradisiacal belly sheltered from the aggressions of the world. This hellish pregnancy was also by the contradictory feelings which animated the mom and which she will deliver to us little by little. She hoped that this child would bring her a new life, but she was not able to imagine the physical, psychological and social constraints that a pregnancy and the care of a baby would impose. So much so that she sometimes felt perse-cuted by these usual inconveniences and ordinary obligations that she would later blame on her baby. Or on the contrary, perceiving at other times her inability to assume them, she then thought herself harmful to the child. "I don't know how I would know how to take care of a baby." This ambivalence of feelings, sometimes mixed, was never foreseeable and the mother oscillated from one day to the next between threats of abduction, disinterest in her daughter, recri-minations towards her baby or an avoidance of her contact when she felt too helpless to answer her needs or when she feared her own violent impulses.

Stress and relational withdrawal

Violette was a quiet baby who was forgotten. She did not ask for her bottle and stayed awake without crying or asking for it. She was very anxious and it took a good month before she made her first emotional demands, which remained difficult to interpret because of the confusion of their expression. During the first weeks, her mothering staff had to make an effort to pay attention to the timid signs of Violette's desire to rest on them. It was difficult to unders-tand her reactions and guess her desire for emotional connection. Her first instinct was always a gesture of defiance before she relaxed and trusted in a second step. Violet was both in relational avoidance and in search of reassurance.

A noise and she retracted, becoming inaccessible to, a time after, finally relax in the arms. If she never tried to hold on with her gaze, she nevertheless came quickly enough to shake the finger of her mothering rather than to contract on herself when she was surprised. When Violet seemed to be absent, not responding to verbal requests, her educator could still see the roll of her eyes under her closed eyelids when she spoke to her. Although she stiffened when she was taken, she would then cuddle up and abandon herself in the arms that carried her. Besides, everything was better when she was carried. She liked to be carried around, held in your arms or in a sling, as if she felt more secure than in her crib.

She appreciated that her mothering took care of her. It was discreet but it had become much more noticeable. Now she would turn to Benedict when he spoke to her, but not to the point of meeting his eyes. She always avoided his eyes and fixed hers elsewhere.

At the time of the first parental visits, Violet was still defenseless, irremediably plunged into great anguish, unable to protect herself from the violence of her mother's paradoxical and contradictory emotions. This one could torment the professionals by shouting that she was going to kidnap her daughter: "It will not be a kidnapping because she is mine! The judge will not say anything, she is my daughter. When she took pictures of her daughter, it was to threaten to file a lawsuit on derisory subjects that had no relation to reality. They were not memories, but evidence for who knows what. Violette existed for her only as the object of a possible litigation.

With the father, they appeared curious, amused, quickly bored and disappointed like the small children who discover for the first time what is a baby, a thing which drinks, which cries and which sleeps and with which one cannot make anything. At the time of the change, Violette was taken of a violent start of the whole body, her four members unfolded then retracted, her back tightened. Instead of trying to calm her down, her parents burst out laughing, which triggered other outbursts: "You saw! She already knows how to do the arm of honor! Did you teach her?" They were watching this baby's reactions but not considering Violet. At that moment, in their eyes, she was just a turtle on her back waving her legs.

In this situation, Violette was alone and nothing and no one could soothe her anguish. She did not dare to cry. She did not yet have the resources to turn to her mothering mothers or to seek them out with a glance. So she put her little hands together and intertwined her fingers, squeezing them tightly. It was not a gesture of supplication, nor a mute imploration, nor even a posture of prayer, but a reflex of self-gripping. It was the only way she could hold on to a helping hand: his. For the first few days after her admission she had had this amazing way of holding on to herself, hands clasped and fingers intertwined, especially during bottle feeding. But she soon traded her own hand for a finger of her mother. So it was very hard for her educators to see Violette sink into chaos so alone again, without being able to do anything to hold on to her, at the very moment when she was just beginning to trust them.

First contacts with humans

It is only at the age of 1 month that Violette addressed her first frank smile. She had just taken her bottle, Benedicte still had her in her arms. "I was talking to her, trying to get her attention and she smiled at me. The first one!" Previously Violette was always evasive or would only catch her eye for a few short moments. If you looked at her too much, she would frown and turn away. At 6 weeks old, she would twist her mouth to try to get some sounds out but could only produce silences. Violet worked hard at this and her teachers pretended to understand these silent statements by encouraging her. She soon discovered that screaming with vigor allowed her to find herself comfortably in loving arms. She calmed down immediately, as if by magic. But it was not until three months later that she no longer observed the big bursts.

Violette learned to connect with and rely on her educators and to use this resource to protect herself somewhat from the sudden and unpredictable outburst of her mother's emotions during visits.

The storm of maternal emotions

Most of the time her parents did not show anything when Violette arrived in her mother's arms. They did not get up, they did not come forward to say hello to Violette. The little one looked at them, suspended, without reacting.

It was as if they were indifferent. Then it was Violet who made the effort to try to relate to them, but it was difficult. Her parents did not smile at her or talk to her. They didn't seem to think that they could have a reciprocal relationship with this baby that they looked at as a strange thing, that lived, ate, cried, smiled sometimes, but with whom they didn't imagine that it was possible to share emotions. The mother, without expression, gave the feeling of looking at something behind a window. It was impossible for her to identify with the child. The reality was probably more complex. This mother was paralyzed by the confusion of feelings that crossed her while observing this baby: demand for love and aggressiveness, claim of possession and indifference or rejection, protective desires and mortifying desires, which transpired from her always hard and raw words.

If Violet falls asleep and doesn't move, she suddenly asks, "Is she dead? Not holding any more anguish after such a thought, she wakes her up by exciting her with a stuffed animal that she walks on her face and then spikes her mouth with a pacifier. When she is offered to take her daughter, she refuses, claiming cold hands, a cold or three cat hairs on her sweater. Violette has gas and squirms to the point of crying, her mother laughs to see her contort herself like that. Violette coughs a lot, her mother then evokes her own diseases, in particular a urinary infection after her childbirth and adds: "It is because of her." She talks about her vomiting in early pregnancy and says, "It's her fault." As she carries Violet in her arms, she tells of being smashed in the head as a child, "Do you know if it's more dangerous for a baby to fall on its head?" Her thoughts, frightening, scrolled continuously and she expressed them without restraint, to make one cold in the back and to give the vertigo.

On her side, in front of this mother parasitized by her thoughts, Violette went to the coal, spent energy but returned her empty bucket. Faced with the absence of answer of her parents, Violette wore a small smile but the tuft of her chin trembled a little. It was as if her eyes were smiling but her cheeks and mouth were close to tears. It was a sort of command smile, a bit frozen. It was hard to predict if her face would brighten or if it would end in tears. Sometimes Violette would even try a frank smile, and then, without returning, she would give up. Violette was as if petrified by the impassivity of her parents. They remained there, sitting on their chairs, and it was necessary to ask them who was going to take Violette: "You madam? You sir?"

To help them, they were advised to show their affection for Violette in a more visible way. The educator invited the parents to come closer. It was "amazing," she reported, "Violette tried to sneak a peek at her mother and then came to take refuge in my eyes."

The next visit, the parents got up to say hello to Violette as soon as she arrived. It was a borrowed gesture, without any real affect, in conformity with the instructions received. Violette was surprised and escaped from their gaze to cling to the eyes of the gentleman, an educator in training, who was accompanying the meeting that day. Violet had only seen him once before. He was stunned and bewildered, not understanding that such a young baby had sought him out, a stranger, a man, a student, a trainee, with no professional experience, no knowledge of babies or fatherhood, rather than her parents. He felt sorry for the parents but could not see himself abandoning this baby to its fate.

Violette learns about the weather

Another visit. Her mother seemed touched as she gave Violette her bottle. But she quickly lost interest in her daughter and started talking about something else with her companion. Violette did not even have time to exchange glances.

Violet was quick to judge the tone of the atmosphere generated by her parents and to find strategies to adapt to it.

When the mother was closed and opposed, mute, when there was tension in the air, Violette played the absentee. She would step aside. If her parents approached her, she would turn her head and might even cry. The father seemed to be a little more adapted and sensitive to his daughter and sometimes managed to calm her down. But he was mostly preoccupied by his friend's reactions that he tried to contain and reassure. When he did not succeed, to avoid an explosion of anger, he took for his own the aggressiveness and the violent words of the mother and made an alliance with her.

When the atmosphere was too heavy, the educator suggested a walk in the stroller. Everyone was distracted by the landscape that passed by at the rhythm of the steps and Violette calmed down well this way. But when the mother wanted to take her back, Violette was in tears.

The distraught mother said, "I can't hear my daughter cry." She seemed very insecure in her confidence that she could reassure her baby.

Other times, if her parents were unavailable, Violet might fall asleep in the middle of the visit and then magically wake up as soon as she left the room when she realized she was going to be reunited with her motherers. But when the visit went wrong, she could cry a lot after the meeting and become stiff and difficult to carry again.

Bénédicte was surprised: "However, with us, she was much more spontaneous. During the care she would laugh out loud. She would call out when she wanted me to take care of her. Her eyes would sparkle and her gaze would light up when I reached out to pick her up."

However, during certain meetings her mother was more relaxed and almost serene. Violette, more experienced on her side, was able to enter into a relationship with her. Mutual glances, smiles and chattering followed. However, Violette always kept in touch with her mother, out of the corner of her eye, just in case. She now knew how to stay connected to a secure terminal.

Violette calms down

From the time she was 6 months old her face softened and she was much less tense. From then on, she always took the initiative in the relationship. According to her mothering staff, "she babbled while waving her arms and legs, stared and was very sensitive to speech. She became very tactile, often holding a finger, wrist or gently touching our earrings for a long time but never pulling or hurting. She was very gentle."

She was a little girl who also listened with great attention, almost seriously. When she became impatient for food or to be picked up she would cry loudly but would calm down as soon as she was satisfied. She became able to take care of herself with her games when she had had her fill of relationships and cuddles. Then she would ask for it a little later, as soon as she felt like it or out of rivalry with another child who had hogged the available knees. When the answer didn't come fast enough for her, she would start screaming. She loved the contact with the other children. She had formed a special bond with a 3-year-old girl, Lola, who was delighted to be able to make her burst out laughing. Lola would say, "Lolette! Lolette! She's laughing! She's laughing!"

Violette expressed her desires with strength and clarity, but without excessive demands. Her emotions were well pronounced and easy to decipher. So much so that she seemed to be able to speak.

A mother once abused and now persecuted by her baby

The mother was no longer as assiduous at the visits, under changing pretexts, but remained very unpredictable. It was impossible to predict what state she would be in, a mixture of silence and aggressiveness or invasive logorrhea. Even when approached with the greatest benevolence, she could feel attacked by the professionals.

It was always difficult to anticipate how she would react, even to good news. The nurse wanted to explain, cautiously, Violette's progress, that she was more relaxed, that she was sleeping better, that she was not startled anymore.

The mother answered: "When I had her in my belly, she was always jumping. One day I went to the carnival, she didn't like the music, she was banging into me and it hurt. I thought I was giving birth."

Her remarks about Violet were always harsh, even tinged with the feeling of being persecuted by this baby.

Violet regurgitates after her bottle. The mother says to her without sweetness: "Well me, it is because of you that I vomited during the pregnancy!"

Violette startles and bumps her head a little against her mother's cheek. The latter reacts with a threatening tone, "You're lucky...", then softens: "I could have been in a lot of pain!"

If Violette stares at her, her mother warns her without kindness: "You saw my earrings! Well, you'd better not pull on them, otherwise..." and, seeming to hold back: "... Otherwise, I'll be in a lot of pain!"

Violette's mother was taken away from her family at the age of 6, far too late for her to escape unscathed. Beyond her personality as a former child who was flayed, limited, aggressive, exasperating, dangerous at times, she could be touching when the lost child she was called, hidden behind those thorny bushes. Placed and moved in various institutions for children and in psychiatric services, she had no memory of all the detours of her journey. She would sometimes question the professionals she encountered at the shelter to try to learn if anyone remembered having known her in the institution or remembered her. "Was it you who took care of me when I was little?"

What will be the future of Violette?

When Violette was 6 months old, the children's judge explained to the parents that after the time of observation and care in the nursery, Violette would be placed in a foster home.

We feared at this announcement some drama, violent crisis and access of despair or a new threat of kidnapping, but to our great surprise, the mother declared us:

"If it's for Violet's sake, we're willing to let her go to foster care."

Violette will soon be 7 months old. Over coffee, we talk with her mothering staff about her evolution since her arrival.

Benedicte laughs and concludes: "We should change her baby picture above her bed. She is smiling and relaxed today. She is very active, full of energy. She loves to play alone or with us. Her look is alive. This serious baby picture does not look like her anymore. She is no longer crumpled like on this picture. She is a child who has become harmonious and gratifying."

Sylvie asks me: "Will she have a happier destiny than her mother?

I answered him.

"I hope so and I'm sure of it. She is not stressed like she was when she arrived. She discovered with you that humans can be reassuring and helpful. This is what allowed her to develop and build herself without too much damage. Left with her parents, the worst would have happened. She would have been very quickly physically abused because the parents were not able to support the constraint and the psychological pressure that represents the concern of having a baby in charge. She would also have been very seriously handicapped in her development and in the structuring of her personality because of the difficulties of her parents to have empathy for her. They are unable to consider Violette as a full human being, endowed with emotions and feelings, and with whom it is possible to have an affective relationship other than by claiming her possession.

They are not responsible for it. They have never known this solicitude for themselves. How could they have invented it in contact with Violette and for her benefit? The feeling of a possible attention of the other for oneself is acquired only by the primordial experience of the first affective connections, from the first days of life. Later is too late.

Now all that remains is to find her a foster family where she can grow up peacefully."

6 - Elouan hopes, depresses, hopes, depresses...

Storm warning

I come to work at the nursery but it is not my home. It is the "Children's House[10]". So I avoid invading their living space. They know me but they are not used to see me in their daily life except in festive circumstances or exceptional occasions. Today I am in a hurry and I am going to break this rule. I have an agenda issue to settle right away with the educators of the team where Elouan is welcomed.

This little boy is 16 months old today.

I lift the security latch, open the door discreetly and enter this unspoiled sanctuary, her living space. Although I try to be as transparent as possible, two piercing eyes spot me in a second. Black look of astonishment. I try to reassure him: "Don't worry Elouan! I am only passing by." Elouan stares at me, makes the lippe, his chin trembles, his eyebrows frown and tears threaten. Aggravating circumstance, Amandine, his mother, leaves him alone, abandoned

---

10. A term used by professionals in the children's home to refer to the facility to the children in it.

on his play mat, to accompany me in the small adjoining office to consult the calendar. I know Elouan's propensity to panic in new situations, in front of people he doesn't know very well or during short separations. I am going to be responsible for putting water back in the fountains of Versailles. Amandine, who has sensed the impending tragedy, calmly and convincingly explains to Elouan that she will return to him very soon without seeming to worry, which surprises me a little, given the recurrence of her collapses in such circumstances.

Five minutes later, our agendas set, I am about to leave the place as clandestinely as when I arrived because I know that a departure can also trigger the sleet.

I have the pleasant surprise to observe that Elouan, all busy with his game, looks at me passing, serene and quiet. If his handcuff doesn't say goodbye, his eyes express it. I cannot refrain from expressing to his educator, in front of Elouan so that he can hear it, my satisfaction to see how much he has acquired new inner security. I had never known him to be anything but sad, clinging to his mother, grumpy or crying. This evolution is a good omen for the near future. Elouan will have to leave us soon to live with his adoptive parents. Elouan does not know them yet, and they, at this moment, do not know that they will soon be chosen to become his parents.

Elouan's basic insecurity

For Elouan, connecting is laborious, the established connection painful and the disconnection traumatic. To meet, an anxiety; to be in relationship, an uncertainty; to leave, a suffering.

A sequence that mirrors the reactions of his mother who, under the exterior of a great assurance, was panicked when she came to visit him, remained anxious to be with him and was always in a hurry to leave.

After a year of hesitation, she has just announced her choice, assumed, to entrust Elouan to the adoption. A courageous decision on her part, a salutary act for Elouan.

She had entrusted us with Elouan twelve months before, with arms and luggage, a real move. It was a real move. It looked like a child drop-off, although she said she was just tired, that she needed to rest for a while and not have this baby to take care of. Elouan was then a little more than 4 months old. His mother had taken very little care of him before, having entrusted him for long periods, days and nights, to nannies, or to "trusted persons", claiming, according to the circumstances, a state of exhaustion or that she could not bear the crying of a baby.

At the beginning, in the nursery, Elouan took refuge in his bubble by looking fixedly, very concentrated, at his hands which he contorted in slow bizarre and worrying arabesques rather than seeking contact with his mothering. He was very observant, suspicious, and would quickly frown when an adult addressed him. When he accepted contact, his educator would be all over him with a sad, penetrating look that he would hold for a long time. "If I connect with you, will you also let me down right away?" he seemed to want to say. He was really pitiful.

But after this first emotion was expressed, he managed to relax, smile and chirp. He had never known emotional stability since he was born, having been carried from babysitter to babysitter, from familiar to familiar. Very quickly Elouan knew how to make himself understood with cries modulated according to the circumstances, different to say that he was hungry or that he was tired or that his bed was becoming heavy. But he would regain his defiance when a teacher who had been absent for a few days returned or as soon as a new face appeared on his territory.

6 - Elouan hopes, depresses, hopes, depresses...

Magnetic connection and dramatic quid pro quo

Soon Elouan learned to connect in an almost magnetic way. Clack! Like magnets! Especially during the feeding when, while his stomach was filling up, he drank with an intense and penetrating look the sweet presence that he was going to draw in the eyes of his mothering all the time of the feeding without taking off. With one hand he clutched a little finger offered to him.

His mother did not want to take him on a home visit. She came to see him several times a week and Elouan tried hard to get in touch with her. But most of the time, his mother's response was uncertain, so Elouan did not get back to her immediately or was put down and ended up dropping out.

The mother did not notice all these efforts, complaining instead about his lack of enthusiasm, and Elouan suffered from it. He was exhausted from the visits.

The mother has just arrived for a parental meeting and is talking with Amandine who is carrying Elouan in her arms. Elouan is attracted by his mother's voice and seeks her gaze but his mother does not pay attention. He changes his position, turns around. Amandine feels that Elouan's body moves towards his mother. Amandine then approaches the mother thinking that she would like to stretch out her arms to take him. Moreover Elouan anticipated this eventuality and leans the top of his body towards his mother, who does not notice it. It is true that he holds his arms stuck to him, as if he was not certain of the success of his attempt. His trunk shows the inclination of his soul while his arms reveal his restraint. In symmetry, the mother keeps her arms crossed and does not outline any gesture towards him. Amandine perceived that Elouan, disappointed, took again his distances towards his mother and that he clung to her.

She thought about it and decided to intervene by telling the mother that Elouan "would most certainly" want her to take him. The mother replies that she doubts it because Elouan did not reach out to her.

"I definitely don't want to force it."

And to Elouan's address:

"How happy I will be when you hold out your arms to me."

Your connection attempt failed. Try again? Give up?

She ends up taking her son. Elouan seems satisfied. He plays with his long black hair and looks her in the eyes. His mother speaks to him with kindness, words well adapted to a baby of this age. At this moment she is really mom. Successful beginning of connection, Amandine is reassured.

But five minutes haven't gone by and the mother shows discrete signs of boredom that she tries to hide. It is her who makes an effort to maintain her attention to Elouan, and Amandine realizes that several times she glances at her cell phone then at the wall clock. She is already elsewhere. Amandine has noticed that she often announces her departure a good fifteen minutes before the end of the visits, giving the impression that she only wants to stay the minimum of time with her son.

Elouan has noticed that his mother has already left and he too goes adrift. He then leaves his mother's eyes and goes to join a luminous reflection on the ceiling. Elouan disconnected himself. His mother says nothing about it but, disconcerted, tries to fill the emptiness which now separates them. She gets up, paces with him in the room. Elouan, who has worked so hard to connect, in vain, lets out a sob. He returns to the luminous spots that dance up there. Amandine observes him, disappointed for him. Elouan, who has felt Amandine's concern on his face, leaves his deserted luminous island and clings to her eyes.

To give more substance to the next visit, Amandine suggests to the mother to come the next time at feeding time. But it will not be her who will be present that day. Instead of Amandine, it will be Anna, whom Elouan does not know very well. She thinks in her heart that it might be better this way: the mother and Elouan will not be able to rely on a familiar presence and will have to get along better.

That day is coming.

Elouan drinks his bottle and stares at his mother. Anna is sitting at a small distance. But soon, having undoubtedly perceived a certain wavering in his mother's attention, his gaze escapes and clicks on Anna's, almost a stranger to him. A twisted situation, like Elouan's body, which is clinging to the bottle his mother is holding and which is glued to the eyes of another. But this is preferable to his usual refuge in the undressed spectacle of the ceiling's light spots or to his escape in bizarre hand games as when he was admitted to the nursery.

"So next time, try to come at bath time."

As for "the emperor, his wife and the little prince [who] came to..." and found the door closed. What will happen tomorrow?

This time, Elouan is quite relaxed in the bathtub, he crosses his mother's eyes several times, but without lingering on it. He is well in his bath and has other things to do. Or maybe he's the one who's already gone? The mother takes him out of the water with tender gestures. She puts him on the changing table. Usually Elouan is in a good mood after his bath, it is a time he likes and where he babbles a lot during the care and the dressing. He seeks again the eyes of his mother who concentrates only on the technical aspects of the situation, the layer, the socks, the clothing, the small knots to be made. In a heavy mutism, on both sides.

Elouan, usually so prolix with his mothering in these privileged moments of care, remained silent.

Connections, disconnections

The educators in charge of this child are alarmed by these perpetual connections and disconnections during visits. The child psychiatrist is called in as a backup with Lucile, our psychologist.

We receive together the mother and Elouan.

I wait with the mom in the meeting room. She is dapper and pleasant. Elouan arrives in the arms of his educator. Elouan looks at his mother as if she were a stranger. This is the impression he gives. In reality, the mother is very changeable in her moods and appearance, one day sophisticated and dressed up, the next day defeated and neglected. The contrast is impressive from one time to the next. Elouan is trying to figure out which mother he is going to deal with today, the one who is very perfumed or the one who is falling apart.

The mother takes her time, looks at her son, asks him if he is happy to see her. But she does not express her own feelings to him and we will not know if she is happy to see him. Elouan finally smiles at her. She takes him in her arms, Amandine leaves the room and Elouan turns to follow her with his eyes when she leaves him. The mother sits down with Elouan on her lap. He turns to look at her. They smile at each other, the mother talks to him attentively. Elouan answers her with lallations. He is so diligent in his effort to communicate that his arms and legs shake a little to the rhythm of her sound messages. All his body is gathered in this impulse of communication towards his mother. Elouan is babbling. At this moment, the mother is able to carry out her exchanges with Elouan and the conversation with us by alternate and fast back and forth of the word and the glance. Elouan talks, she answers him. We comment, she nods. Then she returns to Elouan. It is lively, followed, coherent, no disconnection. A high-speed Internet box supports several connected devices, the television, the telephone and the laptop in WiFi. The hotline is available and efficient. Everything works and you don't get frustrated. The world is within your reach.

This meeting time, medical and psychological, a little solemn, supports the mother in her maternal attention. Elouan takes advantage of it.

It won't last more than ten minutes.

Elouan grabs the collar of the blouse of his mother, in limit of her cleavage, and the back of his hand touches the top of her breast. The mother reacts quickly.

"You undress me!" She then grabs the little hand and pushes it away, without brusqueness but without softness either. I believed for a moment in a reaction of modesty. There was however nothing improper there and the gesture of Elouan would have remained unnoticed because banal, without this sudden reaction. What followed proved to me that it was indeed something else. It was the contact of skin to skin which bothered the mother. This exploration of the adult's body surface is a step that sometimes follows the baby's conversation. The child reaches for hair and earrings, the edge of clothing, a bracelet, watch or necklace. He or she may then want to go and put fingers in the adult's eyes or mouth, which is very intrusive and requires saying "no" at some point. The mother did not wait for this stage and therefore pushed away the hand that was clinging to her collar and had touched her breast.

But to reach this stage of richness of connections, neuronal, cognitive, affective and cultural, there are several steps to respect.

When adults foolishly ask children to "make fun", a polite figure of speech imposed on "well-behaved" babies, which they must perform as a social ritual addressed to complete strangers, they ignore the child's psychic reality. The child is not a small animal to whom one teaches circus acts or to give the paw.

Emotional connection tests

The sequence of connection from a baby to the adult is specific to each infant but always respects a certain logic. The baby launches signals, of opening or closing, which, according to the answer received, will allow or not to pass to the next stage. Like the successive phases of connection of the old modems, verification of the tone, dialing, start of the connection, test of the test pattern, PPP authentication, established connection.

The child's gaze, first of all, staring at the adult. Who is it? Known? Unknown? Good mood? Bad mood? The baby tests the quality of the line. He checks if there is a tone.

Open line. Next step

The gaze is fixed on the adult's eyes. First docking. The child sends a connection request. Positive response. What kind of connection? Tense? Relaxed? Happy availability?

Next step, numbering

Small cheek mimics appear, but no immediate smile. They may evolve into a smile, but it may be of varying color and intensity. Mostly happy and joyful. In babies who are doing well, their eyes crinkle. The smile reflects the entry into a phase of confident and peaceful relationship. But there are smiles of conformity or facade in babies who know that it is better to avoid angering mom or dad. This can even go as far as a dissociation of expression, stern eyes, a constrained smile and a quivering chin. Babies who smile but look like they are going to burst into tears. These do not move on to the next phase.

Next step, start the conversation

A happy baby's smile, received five out of five by the adult, always triggers a verbal response from the latter, which initiates a "conversation" by the baby whose range of sounds will become richer with age. It is characterized at the beginning by a great tension of the look and accompanied by a small body gesticulation, especially of the hands and feet, testifying to a total physical engagement, still badly regulated since its muscular effort, to produce sounds and to control them, diffuses then in all its body.

The connection is established. It will be enriched and developed over the months and will become more complex through reciprocal games, vocal games, body games, manipulative games, all of which are known as "nanny games" and more. The child reached this level of connection is in condition to download, hack, store all the information that he can collect from the adult at a lightning speed. Because of this trusting relationship, the child uses the adult's brain to analyze the world, the environment, the nature of things, the

6 - Elouan hopes, depresses, hopes, depresses...

quality of encounters, the meaning of noises by making his own the experiences and reactions of his emotional support.

You have lost the definition of a word, you ask your mobile terminal and you have the answer in a few seconds. A baby does the same thing, but you are its mobile terminal, which it questions with a look, a frown, a surprise, a brief and quickly reassured cry, a few vocalizations, and you answer it without even realizing it. It's a high-level hacker who has placed a bug in your mind!

Once the child has acquired speech, he or she will not need to make eye contact as much.

Elouan and his mother : dropout

After Elouan's gesture towards his mother and her reaction, the disconnection was complete. The mother tried to take things in hand by means of childcare activities but the previous experiences of iterative disconnections lived by Elouan were not going to arrange the things.

She suddenly picks up her baby and says, "Did you poop?" and decides right away to go change him. No reason. But on both sides the heart is not there any more. Elouan lets himself be changed but no longer finds the look in his mother's eyes as she talks to him without really addressing him. She talks about unimportant things. Lucile, who has accompanied them, perceives that Elouan is as if suspended, looking for a way to cling to his mother who will no longer come. No look, no words, no shirt collar, no warmth of the skin, not even a helping finger. Then Elouan grabs Lucile's finger, fixes his gaze on her and sends her bursts of voice and smiles. The same twisted situation as at the bottle-feeding session. Elouan knows Lucile much less than his mother. After the change, nothing goes as before, Elouan whines, turns away and his mother has to walk around the room to distract him, but nothing works. He lands in Lucile's arms where he calms down instantly.

The mother then gave us technical explanations for her son's malaise, hunger, fatigue, teeth, but she then remarked that each time the situation degenerated, Elouan was more quickly restored in the arms of professionals than in his own.

"Do you think he rejects me?" she then asked me.

Backwards question!

Winter solitude

We met again but the situation did not evolve. She refused any proposal for psychological work to help them both to know and understand each other better, arguing that she was unavailable for work. On the contrary, she no longer came to the visits and refused the telephone calls, making excuses for herself by third parties.

It was at the beginning of winter, in November. Elouan, who was then 1 year old, went into hibernation. He was close to speaking and walking but all his progress froze for several months. A sensitive but joyful and rewarding baby until then, deep dark circles now marked his face, unpredictable mood swings overwhelmed him and his nights were restless. He had become passive, extinct and apathetic, or he would get drunk with loud chants that he didn't address to anyone. And what to say to him? How to explain this desertion?

Four painful months passed. It was a letter that announced the rebirth of life at the beginning of March. The mother had made the effort to write to the Administration to express her intention to entrust Elouan to a family who would be willing to adopt him. A moving and noble letter where she recognized her difficulties to invest this child and that she thought it was better for him to grow up with parents who would love him.

6 - Elouan hopes, depresses, hopes, depresses...

Elouan's spring

It was the swallow that made the spring. The time to consolidate the administrative steps, to announce the news little by little to Elouan, then with solemnity in the office of the inspector of the Child Welfare Office who was just as moved as Elouan. "Your mother can't take care of you anymore. We're going to find you relatives. Your mother thought it would be best for you. She had a lot of courage to decide that. I'll keep her letter in your file so you can read it one day when you grow up."

Very concentrated, Elouan listened to everything the gentleman told him, which he didn't know.

He came back to the nursery, ate well and had a very good night. In the following days he started to talk and walk.

It was there that we met and that I was so surprised by his positive and rapid evolution. Amandine then told me about Elouan's recent progress:

"He loves it when I change the words of the little rhymes and ditties I usually sing to him. When I put "papa" and "mama" anywhere in the text, even if it doesn't make sense, Elouan laughs out loud. And so do I! He says "papa" and "mama" by himself. He sings at night in his bed. But I must tell you that he still plays with his hands sometimes. Does that worry you?"

I guessed from her amused look that Amandine, mischievous, was making fun of me a little.

She added triumphantly, joining gestures to her words:

"Yes! He still plays with his hands but it's to make the puppets when we sing together. And sometimes he does it alone while watching me out of the corner of his eye."

Spring is an excellent season for grafting.

7 - ERIC, ELECTRONIC CHILD

A strange child

Eric is 3 years old. The report from the hospital where Eric was taken is overwhelming. Eric does not speak but makes grunts that no one understands. He is dirty. His body has blue, purple, dirty green, old yellow marks on his neck, behind his ears, on his face, on his chest. But these marks of blows do not correspond to the usual localizations of the bruises which are observed at the time of the training of the walk in the unskilled children, on the lower parts of the body and on the front. These are on the upper body and on the back. Within reach of an adult's hand. The weight of the child is too low for his age.

When he was admitted to the hospital, his mother, who seemed to have some awareness of the child's developmental delay, explained his condition - bruising, emaciation, lack of language, fearful behavior - by the character she attributed to this child: "He is a good-for-nothing. Since he didn't speak, I didn't know when he was hungry or thirsty. He doesn't walk. He bumps into things or falls on the floor, so I left him upstairs, locked in his room. I never put him outside. I'm not very good at giving affection to children, I'm not very comfortable with them. Eric, I couldn't be alone with him. I didn't know how to deal with this boy, it was less dangerous to leave him in his room. But he must have been banging around in his bed, and since he still had bruises on his head, the nursery nurse took him here to the hospital."

In the waiting room of the pediatric emergency room, Eric is prostrate on a chair, vigilant to his mother's every move. She harshly discourages his rare attempts to go to the toy box that attracts him like a magnet: "Come here, you'll fall. It's not yours, you'll break the toys."

Suddenly the mother goes out to smoke a cigarette. She plants Eric there and leaves without a word, without an explanation. Eric takes the opportunity to get down from his chair, to venture into the room and to seek a furtive contact with the people present, whom he does not know. The nursery nurse who had accompanied them answered his gaze. He calls out to her again with little grunts when he manages to manipulate some toys he has taken out of the forbidden box.

The mother returns to make him lunch. No doubt to belie the child's apparent clumsiness and obvious tardiness, she demands that he fend for himself for his meal. "Show that you are a big boy." On the contrary, he shows himself clumsy and very clumsy, which ends up exasperating his mother, seeing the failure of his demonstration. Enraged, she starts to stuff him with brusqueness, without a word. Eric must chew quickly. It is a hot spring day, Eric shows his glass. "When you're done." His mother refuses to let him drink until he has finished his plate, big bite after big bite, at full speed.

She left him after a furtive kiss. She called only once in five days to check on the child. She did not return to visit him. Eric is her third child, his two older sisters were placed in care long before he was born, and their mother had not tried to keep in touch with them, despite requests from social services.

In the pediatric ward, Eric watches in a daze as people talk around him and seems to understand nothing of what is being said. Eric does not communicate but often gets angry when there is nothing in his environment or activity to explain it. He is panicked by the technological noises of this modern hospital, the electronic chime of the elevator at the end of the hall, the jingle of the microwave in the nurses' station, the ringing of the telephone and the many beeps and beeps of all kinds. Even the balloon, placed there in an attempt to brighten up this frightening place and seek to distract from the omnipresent illness, frightens her.

Eric, baby of the closet

The various reports recovered from the social workers are as appalling as the child's condition. Eric has never known anything other than the family home. He doesn't know what a nanny, a crèche, or a daycare center is. He had never left his parents, or rather his mother, for a single day, a single hour. But they did not live together. Eric lived in his bed, in his room upstairs, and his mother on the first floor. On weekends his father would come home from work to his wife.

As soon as the baby was born, concerns arose about the quality of the care provided to the baby by his parents. After two years of administrative and judicial procrastination, family workers were mandated to visit the home. They knew of Eric's existence but never saw him. Eric was confined to his bed one floor up. They could hear him stirring above.

His mother agreed two or three times that he should come downstairs and be introduced to them. He couldn't laugh and would glance at his mother before doing anything. He seemed to fear her. She would deny him her lap and the affectionate gestures he would beg for. She would respond to the visitors' perceptible astonishment by saying that Eric was too big to receive any more hugs. She would call him "the Mongol" or "the Fat Man", which was a bit of a stretch for a child who had been ill-treated because of his lack of affection.

During these encounters, the child externalized a massive relational greed whose uncontrollability exasperated his mother - a fine example of an aborted attempt at selective connection. In fact, he began to hit his bed as soon as he recognized the noises that signaled the weekly visit of these strangers. Faced with these manifestations, his mother refused to allow him to go downstairs to break this nascent habit, and locked him in his room. The parents also exchanged his wooden bed, from which he managed to escape and from which he managed to exploit the resonance of the material to signal himself, for a canvas bed that he could no longer climb to get out. And as a supreme refinement, he got less noise from it. One would think that his parents had understood why dictatorships are so fond of censorship on the Internet or adept at cutting off access to the Web.

The first two years of Eric's life were those of impossible connections and this third year, until his admission to the hospital, that of forbidden connections.

Without an available affective connection, the baby is built in a closed circuit. It is then mounted in a loop

Eric comes to us at the nursery as soon as he leaves the pediatric ward.

He was a strange child.

He had a panic fear of care and bathing but paid no attention to his own protection. He would fall, hit himself, hurt himself but seemed insensitive to pain. He never asked for a kiss or a cuddle, cried without noise, whined without tears and burst out laughing without reason. He was very stressed when he went to his room and only fell asleep when he was exhausted. At first, visitors would have thought they were in a Romanian orphanage during the Ceaucescu era when they saw him rocking in his bed. This was one of the first strange habits he abandoned, helped by the presence of an educator who put a hand on his shoulder. In these moments of extreme inner solitude, he showed himself to be sensitive to human solicitude.

We observed from the moment of his admission that he did not seek out interactions with humans and the living world, but that he was fascinated by electronics, wires, connections, diodes, electric buttons and on-off buttons on household appliances. He wandered into the educators without seeing them, stepped on the bodies of the crawling babies without even noticing them, but rushed in at every opportunity to manipulate the keys of the microwave, the remote control of the television, fiddling with the keys of the telephone. If he heard the dull, faint sound of the refrigerator door opening, he would run to watch the interior light bulb turn on and off. His very limited language was directed only to himself. He used only three sounds that he repeated out of any associated context. These were monotonous melodies: the repetitive alarm of a truck backing up, the continuous tone of a landline and the beep-beep of a busy number. Sometimes it sounded like he was talking, but with his mouth closed.

Chaos inside, chaos outside

He spent the first two years in the nursery, destroying his room, of which he dismantled one by one all the elements, bed, night table, chair, cupboard, painting, until the window and the electric plugs.

In spite of regular repairs, Eric had managed to give it a solitary look, which could suggest the worst about the quality of care in this nursery. Only the mattress resisted. The spectacle of this child in such a bad state, who occupied such a desolate place, earned us some not very friendly remarks reproaching us for the lack of care that we would have had of his person. This room was not only to remind him of a place of seclusion but also to symbolize the emptiness and chaos of his psychic interior. Few people understand the nature and extent of the inner ruin field that inhabits these unconnected children, just like this desolate room.

7 - Eric, electronic child

Each baby makes a representation of the world around her, like Fiona with her grandmother's pendant, to master its flaws. It's a dream world: "Mommy's not here, but she's coming when I want her." "What I don't have now, I'll have later because Mommy thinks of me." And this dream world works well when the emotional connections are of sufficient quality to not disappoint these expectations too much. "I'm hungry. Mom says, "Are you hungry?" She feeds me." "I don't want to be alone. Mom says, "Don't cry anymore. She takes me against her." "I wake up. I want to see Mom. And I make her appear and I smile so proud that I can make her appear like this every time." "I am magic." "I am unable to move alone, to feed myself alone, to survive alone but I am the creator of the world because I make happen what I need." "I think of the thing and bam! it happens." "I am a magical baby!"

The magical powers of baby's mind

So for a well cared for baby, everything in the world is in its place. Mom before the end of a soft cry. Daddy when I cry at night. The pacifier at the end of the bottle. The mattress on the bed. The chair next to the table. The sunbeam on the wall.

For Eric, the things of the world were not connected to each other. For him, thinking did not make anything appear. The order of the world made no sense, nor did the objects in his room. What difference was there for him between a whole closet and a closet in pieces? There was no difference. He did not break things, he let them return to their original state of primitive soup.

One day, during nap time, he managed to sneak out by lifting the roller shutter of the window, which was quite high. Panic in front of the deserted room. Incredulity. How could he get out? Where did he go? All hell broke loose. He was found on the opposite side of the building, taped to the luminous screen of the photocopier. "I turn on, I turn off. I turn on, I turn off. I turn on, I turn off. I turn on, I turn off. I am not in control of anything in the world, but I am the master of the copy machine button."

Because this light turns on and off when he commands it. No one came to meet his needs in his room at his parents' house. Eric had not yet understood that it could be different with other humans.

Eric spends many long hours opening and closing a door. He listens to the sound, observes its movement. He is fascinated by the borborygms of the water flowing down the drain of the sink. His own gurgling sounds worry him a lot: "I don't want frogs in my belly."

Eric snatches the television remote control. He strips it and extracts black sticks, the batteries. He becomes fascinated by batteries and tries to dismantle all objects likely to contain them. A dead beetle on the doorstep: "A pu pile? A sound book: the story does not speak to him, does not interest him, he wants to see the battery. A cartoon is proposed to him: he seems to agree, but it is to make the record go in and out of the turntable ad infinitum.

He is on the lookout for any light to be turned off or on, ready to run away to handle extension cords to be plugged and unplugged. At the garden center, in front of the aquariums, he is captivated by the bubbling pumps and is not interested in the multicolored and shimmering spectacle of the fish.

Of living beings, he perceives only partial aspects, just as the battery is only a part of the remote control. Some days, Bernard, our gardener, takes him to see the chickens. Eric does not try to attract them by giving them seeds that are offered to him. He has only one idea, which obsesses him: to take a feather from them, which he plucks. After the pile, the feather. In spite of multiple unsuccessful warnings, we decided to protect the hens. No more trips to the henhouse.

Eric looks at a newly arrived baby: "Where is the battery?" Eric eats a pancake, sees the pacifier in the baby's mouth, removes it and shoves his pancake in its place without even looking at him or saying a word. It is likely that he himself has been force-fed this way.

Faced with such a behavioural disorder, medical examinations were scheduled to rule out a brain-related cause. Eric went for a skull X-ray. He had to remain absolutely still. It was an unlikely task to get such an elusive child to do so. Yet Eric stood still, like a statue of salt, earning the admiration and amazement of the two lady radiologists at his wisdom and obedience. "You're so cute." It's true that, in addition, he's a beautiful child. They didn't realize that Eric had taped his eyes to the little red light that was flashing in front of him. Continuing the misunderstanding and wanting to reward him for his performance in wisdom, they invited him to join them behind the leaded windows. "Come see your picture!" Eric was fascinated by the bright screens and desks covered with buttons. Quick, agile and elusive, he managed to get everything out of order in no time. The ladies didn't understand this sudden change at all.

Don't give in to chaos: repairing is healing

When we lamented his condition and the state in which he was reducing things, he replied: "Gildas will fix it. Gildas will repair." And Gildas, the man with the skilful hands, came, repaired, patched up, reassembled and remedied everything, without getting angry. Breaking his room and the rest made Gildas appear. Magic!

This consistency in caring for Eric and the things around him eventually paid off. Gildas surprised him by building a bed in the shape of a car. A magnificent work, a unique piece: Eric's bed - the feet in the shape of wheels were solidly fixed to the ground, the bottom of the bed simulated a grill. From then on, Eric was able to live in this place and he invited objects to come and live with him. Finally, this room no longer looked like a ramshackle prison cell but like a little boy's room. He invited me, all proud, to come and visit it. "Gildas! Bed! Car!" I entered, I admired, but he had already flown away.

We thought he was also beginning to build an inner world, which was gradually emerging from a field of ruins. When Eric was five years old, his teacher told him a picture story and Eric was surprised by the funny situation of pigs climbing a tree. Eric disagreed with the picture: "It's not normal. Pigs are on the ground. Not in trees."

He was about to turn 6 and was finally able to question his place in the world and worry about whether anyone was waiting for him anywhere. Seeing other children going into foster care, he asked our department head. "Me go where next? I want a home. Me foster care."

This is a very difficult wish to fulfill for children as damaged as Eric, given the severity of their behavioral problems. They can destroy the balance of a family as surely as Eric had ruined his room.

Can a closet baby survive?

Can a baby grow and develop without connections with humans? This is a very old question to which history provides very contrasting answers depending on the era.

James IV of Scotland (1473-1513), believed that language came spontaneously to children. He therefore imagined a simple way to verify what was the original language of humanity, a natural and universal language that would have existed before Babel. In reality, he was only repeating the previous experiments carried out by other rulers who had tried to find out in which language infants would express themselves after two years of a strict regime depriving them of all human speech.

At the time of James IV, history claimed that these babies raised by mute nannies would have spoken Hebrew.

Before him, Frederick II of Hohenstaufen (1194-1250) emperor of the Holy Roman Empire and king of Sicily, had tried the same experiment with forty infants, all of whom died!

"Frederick II] wanted to conduct an experiment to find out what the language and idiom of the children would be when they reached adolescence, without them ever having been able to speak with anyone. Thus he ordered the nurses to breastfeed the children [...] and not to speak to them. For he wanted to know whether they would speak the Hebrew language, which was the first, or the Greek, or the Latin, or the Arabic; or whether they would always speak the language of the parents from whom they were born. But he took pains without result, because the children or newborns all died. (Salimbene de Adam de Parme, *Cronaca* [Chronicle], xiii century.)

James IV and Frederick II, both great scholars, had undoubtedly read Herodotus, and had tried to reproduce the experience of the pharaoh Psammetichus I (about 663-609 BC): *"Before the reign of Psammetichus, the Egyptians believed themselves to be the most ancient people on earth. But when Psammetik became king, he wanted to know which people really deserved this title; and since that time, the Egyptians think that the Phrygians preceded them, if they are themselves more ancient than all the other peoples. All the researches of Psammetichus to discover a way to learn which people was the first to appear on earth having remained vain, he imagined this procedure: he had a shepherd give two newborns, children of the common people, to bring up in his stables under the following conditions: no one, he ordered, was to pronounce the slightest word in front of them; they were to remain alone in a solitary hut, and at the desired hour the shepherd was to bring them goats and give them milk to their fill, as well as all the necessary care. With these measures and orders, Psammetichus wanted to catch the first word that the children would utter when they had passed the age of inarticulate wailing. And so it was; for two years the shepherd did his work, and then one day, when he opened the door and entered the hut, the children dragged themselves towards him and pronounced the word becos, holding out their hands to him, which is, among the Phrygians, the name of bread. The Egyptians bowed to such evidence and recognized that the Phrygians were more ancient than they."*

But others thought that the infants had only imitated the bleating of the goats with their cries.

The chronicles tell us about a last experiment of this type, left to posterity under the name of Gang Mahal ("the house of idiots"). It was attempted by Akbar (1542-1605), the Great Mogul. In August

1582, after two years of observation, he came to the conclusion that none of the newborns he had deprived of the musicality of human language had received the talisman of speech and that, in addition, they had become idiots[11].

Forty dead, some idiots, some overlapping and some who would have spoken Hebrew or Phrygian, which remains doubtful.

Dramatic results.

11. Catrou (François), *Histoire générale de l'empire du Mogol depuis sa fondation, on the Portuguese memoirs of M. Manouchi,* 1708.

8 - THERE IS NO SINGLE MOTHER

The maieutic allegory of the Russian dolls

On my return from Siberia, some friends gave me seven Russian dolls of decreasing size, nested one inside the other. It was while I was working on this book, in front of this string of pregnant women lined up on the shelf of my library, that I understood its deep symbolism. They looked at me in amazement every time I looked up from my computer. They all seemed to be telling me the same thing, even the youngest one: there is no such thing as a single mother. Indeed, a mother needs to be surrounded to be able to surround her child. It is absolutely necessary for her to have quality affective supports, whoever they may be, partner or father, friendships, but also the real or internalized support of previous generations. If these supports work, this mother will be relieved of worrying about herself. She will then be able to devote herself to her baby, who will be able to connect with her.

These are also exceptional situations because of their configuration that can make this phenomenon visible to us, whereas in the everyday life of ordinary families, where it works without our even noticing it, we have less visibility of it.

Kelly, neglected child of a mother who was herself neglected

Kelly, 2 1/2 years old, has just been admitted to the nursery. She speaks poorly and makes herself understood by signs. She is handicapped by being seriously overweight and is not helped by her squinting eyes, especially one. She is on the verge of losing the vision of this eye that does anything. Her vaccinations are not up to date. She is throwing tantrum after tantrum, for no intelligible reason. She has only known pasta, rice, sweets and cheap industrial food. Delayed language, overweight, untreated risk of blindness, behavioral problems. The picture of a physically and psychologically neglected child whose health is not good and who has not benefited from any coherent medical follow-up.

I receive her parents. The mother, in a narrative interspersed with silent tears, explains to me that she understands well why the judge made the decision to place Kelly.

"It's a heartbreaker to know that she's at home, but it was the only way. We were so high on pot, morning to night, night to morning, that we didn't even care about the basics. Kelly, she had to breathe a lot of hash vapor. The races, to get up in the morning, the appointments at the doctor's, one forgot everything, one did nothing more. The placement of Kelly, that was an electro shock. Since then, we decided to stop using pot.

The father, still young but already quite ravaged, nods and adds:

"And then it couldn't go on like this. We were spending half the budget on joints. We even did a little dealing at times. It got bad and we had to move. It sucked too much with the big dealers."

The mother cries again:

"When she was crying or angry, Kelly would never listen to me. When she was hurting herself, I couldn't calm her down, and I couldn't calm her down if she was throwing a tantrum. No matter how much I said, it was as if I were a voice on the radio. She couldn't hear anything. It was a circus at home, the kids did what they wanted. Her little brother and I would fight and bite each other like puppies. Since we were always in the coal mine, we couldn't stop them. Sometimes Kelly would sit alone in her corner of the house for hours. I don't know what she was doing. We would get high. I never thought I'd get this low. My parents, they didn't care about me. When I was 13, I only went to school one day out of three, and when I was 14 I didn't go at all. That's when I started smoking joints. They didn't care that I stopped going to school and that I was doing drugs. They didn't lift a finger, they did nothing. And he, Kelly's father, is the same. Except that he started smoking hash when he was 11.

Kelly's difficult relationship with her parents

The first reunion proved to be conflicting between Kelly and her parents. The mom was overwhelmed by her own feelings. She was in the eager expectation to see her daughter again and in the terrible apprehension to have to manage her angers. Troubled by this internal confusion, she could neither welcome, nor recognize, nor channel the little one's emotions.

These visits always followed the same scenario.

Kelly cried as her parents arrived. Was it relief at seeing them again or anxiety at knowing what state they would be in? Tears of joy and sobs of worry. If tears are sometimes a soothing lotion on the pains of life, these had the effect of vinegar on a wound.

The mother, her own feelings confused, did not hear anything with these cries and saw there only caprice, distance and refusal.

"It's seeing me that makes you cry? It's worth it! It's heartwarming!"

Nevertheless the mother tried to pull herself together. She changed her tone. Her voice became soothing. She sought to take Kelly to cuddle her and reassure her. She tried to show her empathy.

"Come on, calm down! I'm glad to see you. Come give mommy a hug."

It was a waste. Kelly would stay locked in her trip and go into a tailspin. If the mom made a step towards her, Kelly pushed a dull cry, turned around and ran to rush in the arms of her educator. The father, who had been standing back, would try to take control of the situation.

"Kelly! Kelly! Come to Daddy!"

She would stomp around in her teacher's arms and didn't want to hear from her parents. Some days it was better. It was hard to deal with this mess of conflicting family interactions.

The attention given to the child cares for its parents

Kelly's distressing condition required numerous medical appointments. Her parents were invited to attend. While they had previously forgotten to comply with these obligations for their child's well-being, they were always present and on time, come hail, snow, rain or shine.

It is Noëlle, the nurse of the nursery, who drove Kelly to her consultations at the hospital. Thus she was also always present with the parents in these regular reunions with their daughter, punctuated by the care which they had not ensured in time.

It is the day of the exams for his eyes.

In the waiting room, the meeting between Kelly and her parents starts on the same rails. Desire to find themselves and reciprocal recriminations.

Noëlle speaks gently to Kelly and invites her to greet her parents. But the hospital universe and the stakes of the consultation do not arrange anything. Kelly perceives the anguish of her mother and defends herself.

Noëlle crouched to be at Kelly's height and to encourage her to go towards her parents. Kelly looks at them one moment then tries to snuggle in Noëlle's neck. This one must contain the push of the little one who arches against her shoulder. She almost is knocked down. Noëlle relativizes, tries to soothe Kelly and to reassure her parents.

At the invitation of her father, half leaning towards her, Kelly turns half and throws a quick glance at her. Black.

Kelly doesn't reject her parents so much as their anxiety and awkwardness.

The consultation is difficult for the mother who holds back her tears when she understands that Kelly is about to lose the use of her eye.

"I knew we should have done something when she was smaller. Is there still hope?"

The ophthalmologist is not reassuring.

"Yes, but it is not won. The situation is critical. She will have to stay several months with the other eye intermittently hidden. This one has to get back to work. Filling one eye is very uncomfortable and requires a cooperative child. With a temperamental child like your daughter, it will be very complicated to get her to accept it."

Nevertheless, little by little, Kelly, taking advantage of the soothing educational environment of the nursery, got better, her parents were less stressed and their relationship improved. The little one made real progress in language and her mother was very proud of it. She told her so, a compliment that made Kelly feel good. Undoubtedly a beginning of exit of the vicious circle of incessant reproaches. Her mother then made attention to notice her progress and congratulated her daughter who returned it well to her by being much closer to her.

Mom once told us:

"I am proud now, Kelly listens to me during visits. She obeys me more often. She can be very nice. I didn't know that before. And then I feel like a real mom because I can calm my daughter down in my arms when she's grieving, which I could never do before."

But she remained torn between the pain of seeing her children little and the satisfaction of knowing they were finally growing up well. She had become aware of her previous failings and their consequences.

Rearrange the Russian dolls in the right order

The various medical care were so many occasions for the parents to follow the evolution of Kelly. They became attached to Noëlle, the nurse who was always there, always constant. Thanks to her presence, they were reassured and participated with interest in the various consultations, which they would never have succeeded in doing alone. They were relieved that the care was well organized and felt gratified to be recognized as Kelly's parents by being involved.

A small and almost comical episode explains this point and how the Russian doll principle works.

It is the day to go to choose the glasses at the optician. An important step because Kelly must absolutely wear her eye filling with regularity. All that can contribute to it is essential and the ceremonial of the choice of the frames takes there a particular strategic value in this context of a difficult child.

With the model selected and the color chosen, the parents are just as excited as Kelly about this purchase. Real kids. It is necessary to notice that this attribute put on the nose of their daughter is from now on the tangible proof, what any observer can verify *of visu*, that she is finally well looked after. The mother is extremely proud of it. She has made this achievement her own as a mother's work, helped and supported in this task by the discreet but persevering presence of the nurse.

The father and the mother shake warmly the hand of the optician, a little surprised by these unusual effusions, then embrace the hands of Noëlle and thank her thousand times for all that she made for Kelly. Until then the mom had not succeeded in being a worthy mother and there, by the miracle of the glasses, she sees herself as a mother in the eyes of the others.

However, there is no guarantee at this point that the treatment will be successful.

On the way home, Noelle witnessed a small scene that showed both how much this mother had become aware of her role as a mother and the sudden need to share this emotion with the previous generation. Kelly's mother was then overwhelmed by the imperious duty to testify of her success to her own mother and her mother-in-law.

She turned on her cell phone and tried to call her own mother, who did not answer.

He had to find someone else to say his pride. It couldn't wait!

Failing that, she called her mother-in-law - no more reliable than her mother, but that's not the point of our story - to whom she explained as if it were a momentous event:

"I took Kelly to the eye doctor because she was squinting. She has to wear glasses every day. We got her some nice frames. Her eyes will get better. I'm so glad we did this. It's about time."

This example sums up the Russian doll principle, this interlocking of generations. In Kelly's case, the mother had no family support. To the blatant absence of concern of Kelly's grandparents for their own daughter, was added the incapacity of the father to support her in her role of mother, if it is not by supplying her with joints with regularity. In the absence of any support, not having known what maternal care was for herself, she was unable to assume her role as a mother to Kelly.

You can't speak a language naturally if you haven't been bathed in it.

What do humans pass on from generation to generation?

It is definitively admitted today that the maternal instinct does not exist in the human species. The maternal function, whose various aspects (affection, attention, the care that a mother must bring to her baby) can be exercised just as well by the father, is an acquired and transmitted competence. This transmission is not an intellectual or learning process but the result of a lived experience. Books, teachings or demonstrations are ineffective in transmitting its essence. They are reminiscences of emotions and experiences that date from long before words. It is a skill that is acquired through contact with other humans by emotional permeability at the earliest age of life. Indeed, each one receives the psychic stigmata of it, like a psychological dot[12] , during the period of very particular affective connection of the first eighteen months of the child. This emotional connection is characterized by the experience of empathy with others, by the sharing of emotions and by the resulting sense of security for the baby. It is vital for the baby to experience this. It is the most precious thing that humans pass on. From generation to generation.

In Kelly's family situation, the professionals who intervened, and in particular the nurse, substituted for a time for the deficient members of the family circle, first with Kelly, then with her mother. They occupied, in a way, for a time, a place of grandparental and parental guardians. This prosthesis, a temporary substitution, was effective. The professionals played the Russian dolls and were first concerned about Kelly, then in cascade, supported the mother, who was then able to carry the child. The mother, thanks to this support, was somewhat restored in her maternal function and she took pride in it. Pride is the first of the maternal emotions. And she had to share this emotion in an imperative way. It was then that she tried to re-establish, with her telephone, the natural connections that should have existed in her family. Illusory attempt undoubtedly but which reveals that this mom had, thanks to the "carrying" of the professionals, repositioned herself in the succession of the generations in her place of mother towards Kelly. The ribambelle on the

-----

12. I voluntarily use this term in the masculine form, as it was in Old French (until the SEVENTEENTH century), to distinguish this notion from both gift, donation and endowment and to give it the dimension of an inheritance received from another generation, while differentiating it, by the use of the masculine form, from the traditional transmissions of material goods during matrimonial unions, which still exist, in new and varied forms, in contemporary times.

shelf had been reorganized with a few intruders, but in good time, in the collection.

That's what was important to this little girl. It was essential that Kelly receive the emotional expression of a proud mother, even if she was not able to take care of her on a daily basis.

Each generation must support and contain the next. When this does not exist, solidarity, love, friendship, social and professional solidarity can and must take its place. Each one of them carries within itself the seed and the dimension of solicitude for the other, which is the very essence of the maternal function.

There is no single mother.

One of the paradoxes of this story lies in the fact that a child placement, well accompanied by competent professionals, can allow parents to become proud of being parents, even though they are separated from their child.

Rayan and his young mother

Another story, that of Rayan, tells of the need to have experienced a positive affiliation with elders in order to be able to become an emotional anchor for one's child.

When Rayan was born, his mother was only 16 years old. His grandmother felt that her daughter was not capable of raising him and decided to take care of him. She took her daughter and grandson into her home and took such good care of them that she gradually pushed the child's mother out of the house. She finally kicked her out of her house and forbade her to come back and hang out. Rayan's mother turned to the social services, who negotiated unsuccessfully with the grandmother, who shut the door in their face. They then turned to the juvenile court judge. A few months later, this one ordered the placement of Rayan in the nursery, after intervention of the maréchaussée at the grandmother's place. The judge specified in his order that he gave mission to the nursery to carry out detailed observations on the capacity of this young girl to take care of her son and that he awaited a precise report on this point.

The mother, let's call her Giovanna, because of her young age, put all the adults in the same bag: persecutors of the youth and robbers of children. She presented herself as a rebellious, casual teenager, sometimes silent, sometimes insolent, then tutting with green and hard words. She would never have given a smile or even a glance to the professionals who had taken over from her mother in the kidnapping of her son. Nothing but sellouts and collaborators. Let them give her child back, period.

Rayan was a small boy who had developed well but was sad and listless. He had a blank stare and showed no emotion. He didn't know much about his mother from whom he had been separated for several months. Giovanna didn't know what to do with him either. And the grandmother's definitive oracle about his supposed inability to be a mother cast a dark and heavy shadow on their early relationship. Always, good and bad fairies pour out on mothers before bending over the cradles.

Stormy and tense beginnings

Giovanna came to see Rayan at the nursery. Our head of service proposed a short meeting to prepare this reunion and to organize the framework of the visits, schedules, regularity, support of a meal, of an activity. The judge had not given the mother a blank check. It was not desirable for Rayan that the imposture of a family abduction be followed by insecurity and anarchy in his daily life. Giovanna gets angry and sends Anna, our head of department, into a tizzy. She just wants to be with Rayan and to be left alone. And to come when she has decided.

- The frame! Frame! Do I look like I should be framed?

- I hear what you're saying, but put yourself in your son's shoes. He needs to know in advance when you will be there and when you won't be. The nursery workers can then reassure him. Mommy will come in two sleeps, in one sleep, after nap time. If not, he will still be waiting and worrying. Will mommy come? Mommy will not come? And we, what will we be able to answer him without lying to him? Of course, Rayan, right now is the day and time of Mom's visit, but today she may have decided that it's tomorrow. Your mother imposed her tyranny on you and Rayan and now you want to subject your son to your whim. The judge has given us the mandate to help you get back together with Rayan and this is not to authorize you and us to do anything.

Giovanna leaves, slamming the door.

Anna will ask one of her colleagues, Danny, for help to take over.

"I think with me, it's over. I'm toast. I definitely fall into the same category as his mother."

Danny, who takes care of Rayan on a daily basis, goes out to talk to the mother.

"Hello! I told Rayan you were coming, he is waiting for you. It would be a shame to disappoint him."

Grunting and sulking.

Giovanna finally decides to come to see her son with Danny. Giovanna and Rayan do not know how to communicate between them. The visit is very poor and Danny does not dare to intervene more for fear of braking a little more the mom. It was still necessary to take time to tame it.

Knowing how to read what is shown in reverse

Next visit.

Giovanna and Rayan don't know what to do together. The mother texts and Rayan plays in his corner. She doesn't talk to him and he doesn't go to her. If Danny has the misfortune to dare to emit a small idea or a light council, Giovanna tackles her seriously. Rayan seeks rather the presence of Danny than that of his mother, which does not seem to offend her. She goes out to smoke outside without warning Rayan.

But Giovanna came back with regularity the said days, for these strange meetings where, according to the appearances, nothing happened. Danny remained there, all in discretion.

In this smooth flow, suddenly Rayan's anger. It was at the very end of the visit, just as his mother was taking him back to his living unit and saying a perhaps more empathetic goodbye than usual. Indeed, after the other meetings, she usually left without warning, from one moment to the next. This time Rayan refused to answer his mother's goodbye. On the contrary he struck it hard of the hand, struggled in his arms and rolled on the ground. Giovanna, disconcerted by this incomprehensible burst, collapsed too and isolated herself from the children.

"What's the point of me coming to the visits? He doesn't give a shit about me. He never turns to me. He plays with you much more than he plays with me. He doesn't need me at all. You know that, you're the one who talks to him and he listens to you. And if I try to be more attentive, to say goodbye nicely, he throws a tantrum. You can see that. He hits me, he rejects me. He doesn't like me. He doesn't want to see me. My mother was right. I'm really just a piece of shit to my son."

Sitting on the floor, with her head in her lap, Giovanna sobbed loudly in the bathroom of the living unit. The rebellious teenager was now just a fragile and bruised little girl.

Danny tries to talk to her. Giovanna, in this circumstance, agrees to listen to him.

"Today Rayan threw a tantrum because it was hard for him to leave you. Even though you don't know how to communicate and be together yet, Rayan has noticed your regularity and your assiduity to the visits. He asks when it's Mom's day. He understands that he is important to you. You don't know how to tell him and he doesn't know how to answer you. But today he was sad that you were leaving. And he didn't know how to express it other than with this anger."

Danny brings in Rayan suddenly calmed down:

"Rayan, you threw a tantrum because you were sad to leave Mom. But you see, your mom is also sad to leave you."

They can then part soothingly but emotionally.

A mother must be emotionally secure to provide security for her baby

Rayan had made a place for Giovanna. Giovanna existed for Rayan.

"You won't be able to be a mother." The grandmother's oracle was belied.

For the mother, it was the occasion of a 180o turn. Her attitude changed dramatically. She became attentive to what Danny was telling her, and then opened up to the other professionals, even the "sold out" and "collabos". She took support on them to go towards Rayan. She had found her place in the ribambelle of the Russian dolls. To be supported and to be surrounded to contain and carry Rayan and to let him reconnect to her.

Now Rayan, previously an emotionless child, cried every time his mother left. The end of the visits were full of emotions and the occasion of negotiations between Giovanna and her son. Little by little, she learned to manage the separations, to take her time, that of the child, without leaving like a thief.

Giovanna began to confide in me about the worries she had during the kidnapping of her child by her grandmother:

"I was always terrified of my mother. She never hurt me with blows, but she always broke me, denigrated me. She called me incapable. And since it was in a climate of violence it was impossible to think of wanting to oppose. She only physically abused the boys. For her, they were the only ones who had value. But she would beat them. She tied my brothers to the radiator. It was for the example. We girls were like butter, but we didn't move a muscle. We were too scared.

Then imagine when Rayan found himself alone at her place. The anguish, the stress that she would end up doing the same with him. My mother is a fury. I had to get him out of her house. I didn't know how, but I had to. I thought that the judge was going to give Rayan back to me and that was that! But my son was placed in a home. I took it very hard. My mother said that I was incapable and so did the judge, because he had placed him there. And I thought you felt the same way.

Giovanna becomes a mother

The mother had everything to learn but progress was rapid. It was soon envisaged that Rayan could spend some days at his mother's, then one day and one night, until he could alternate three days at his mother's and four days at the home. A sort of alternating custody.

The mother was lucky enough to find a partner who supported her while respecting the work she was doing with the home. He also helped her cut ties with her family. She gradually gained confidence in herself but used Danny as a maternal resource until she could stand on her own two feet. Everything from birth control to authority, from dietary rules to weekly menus, from grocery shopping to using the freezer. She also confided her worries and fears that her nieces and nephews would be mistreated and her sadness at not having had a real family life.

A funny episode: Giovanna told about her experience of freezing a cucumber that ended in a complete failure when thawed.

Leaving his mother is becoming more and more painful for Rayan. A two weeks stay, during the school vacations, is scheduled at his mother's place. A few days before, Giovanna is not well. She seems very anxious and her arms are covered with eczema. Danny is worried and tries to understand. Giovanna admits then that she did not dare to say that she did not feel yet ready for such a long period alone with Rayan, without support, her friend being on the move.

She made the decision to give up. The next try, two months later, will be a success.

Then it will be the definitive departure with the regular then spaced passage of Danny at home. Giovanna goes so far as to ask her what she thinks of a baby project. " Now, is it too early for me and for Rayan? "

Today Rayan is about ten years old. Danny met him in a supermarket with his mother and his little sister. The mom has changed her look. She doesn't look like she did at 17 years old, suffering and flayed. She is a pretty, assertive and calm young woman. They exchange some news of the children, of the life. Everything is going well. With her partner, they have just bought a house, which is quite an event.

Rayan listens quietly. Danny introduces himself.

"You don't remember me but I took care of you and your mom when you were a baby. Life was not easy at that time for your mom. I am very happy to see that you are all doing well today."

There is no single mother.

Jean-Jacques Goldman sang about the difficulty:

She calls me when she's sick
When she can't sleep
I take her to the movies, I hug her, I make her laugh
A little like a big brother
A little incestuous when she wants
Then her kid is almost mine, except that he has blue eyes
She made a baby all by herself

9 - CONNECTION FROM BEYOND THE GRAVE

A dead baby

An obstetrician colleague calls me to come and visit a woman in labor urgently.

"Dead," he sees fit to add.

"Dead?" On the spur of the moment, in a split second, several professional stories where birth and death had intersected at the speed of light telescoped in my head. That newborn we had received after his mother had committed suicide near his crib in the maternity ward by asphyxiating herself with a plastic bag. Another who had survived a day and a half in the blood of his mother, murdered by the child's father. A colleague whom I thought very highly of, who hanged himself the day his son was born.

I probably paused for a moment with the phone hanging in my hand and my colleague who realized this adds to reassure me, "She's as good as dead."

I go to the maternity ward. In the on-call room, the midwife offers me a coffee and explains the "case". She is a very keen observer and always has extraordinary stories about the women who gave birth to me each time I come. It is a pleasure to listen to her and to be led from surprise to surprise.

I consult the file.

Mother for the second time, married, well educated, intellectual profession. No known psychiatric history. Last night she gave birth to a beautiful little girl who is perfectly healthy. But the mother no longer speaks, is incontinent, keeps her eyes closed, does not respond to any solicitations, not even those of her husband. She lies inert, motionless as a corpse, but the doctor who examined her did not discover any disorder. She breathes, her heart beats, she is not in a coma. However, she did not react at all to the comings and goings of the maternity ward staff who were busy responding to her baby's first cries and providing the necessary care.

Before sinking into this state, she was able to declare that she was dead.

His transfer to a psychiatric hospital seems to be the only reasonable outcome, the family seems to agree and I am mandated to organize it.

Between catafalque and cradle

I go to the room.

What a strange mission for a child psychiatrist to go and listen to a dead woman!

It is a "chic" maternity ward. The room is bright, the walls light pastel. The baby sleeps peacefully in a transparent cradle. His mother is motionless, lying on her back, arms at her sides, in a spotless bed. There are no wrinkles or folds that could betray any sign of life. The sheets bear no trace of crumpling that might have revealed some insignificant movement. I lead the living out of the room and sit in a chair next to the bed.

I silently watch over a body in a death chamber, immaculate shroud. But, curiosity, a newborn is sleeping next to the dead woman. I am there, between life and death, it is a mystery. Before breaking this disturbing calm, I collect myself, I immerse myself in this little girl and her mother whom I look at in turn, each isolated in a different world. None of them pays me any attention. An improbable scene and I am not in the cinema. Funny function that of child psychiatrist, going back and forth between life and death, crossing the Styx and coming back.

A voice from beyond the grave

In a calm and quiet voice, without forcing myself - to make myself heard by the one who is dead without waking up the one who is alive - I introduce myself, explain my mandate, to have her transferred to a psychiatric environment, but I add that all this intrigues me, that I would be very curious to understand something about it before organizing her transfer. Pride of knowledge of the clinician. No answer, I stay there, I keep silent. The baby is sleeping, the room is pale grey, the linoleum apple green, a strange color. I look at my watch. I perceive, muffled, noises of passage and voices in the corridor. The melodious trills of the birds in the park reach me through the window. It is the hour of my meal break: in my belly, which does not care about death, frogs gurgle. Life. In the room, no noise. To fill this deadly void and the boredom that creeps in, I talk about the baby, a beautiful little girl, really! What time is it? I look at my watch again. I certainly add banalities. I am always very talkative, even with the dead. Before going to give my verdict I wait a little longer.

Always silence, but attentive. Then suddenly the lips of the dead woman speak to me from beyond the grave. Nothing else moves but her lips. She starts to tell me about the deaths of her family, recent deaths. Her parents, two years before, then, last year, her uncle and aunt who had replaced them for a while. All of them were cut down too quickly, in such a short time, lightning diseases, road accidents.

The eldest of five siblings, the previous generation gone, she finds herself *mater familias in* spite of herself. She assumes her role, works, mourns, settles family conflicts and inheritance problems during her pregnancy.

A newborn baby was born, the cycle of life was finally taking its course. She thought she could see the end of the tunnel. But today, she is the one who is dead. Well, not quite, and three times a day, for three days, I will come and sit there and listen to her, while she starts to take an interest in her pretty little girl. Psychiatric hospitalization is no longer on the agenda, she leaves the maternity ward with a few safety instructions to her husband. She will then come to my office for several months to continue to talk to me about the living and the dead, and about her baby, who is doing just fine.

What happened in that room when I sat on that seat between a catafalque and a cradle, between a living woman in suspense and a dead woman who had lost her speech, so that suddenly life came back and the connections were re-established one after the other like after a power cut?

A little anthropology

Let's take an anthropological and historical detour.

In ancient times, the Greeks called *amphidromia* the ceremony that consisted in welcoming the child into the family and giving him a name. The Romans called this celebration *aspersio* or *lustratio*. Between five and eight days after birth the newborn child, who had survived the uncertainty of the first days of life and whom the *pater familias* had decided to raise, was taken around the house and presented to the domestic cult of the hearth and the ancestors. The hearth was a domestic deity in itself that demanded that it be honored and fed. The hearth probably represented in the ancient family group the distant symbol of the domestication of fire during prehistory. Its presence under the family roof marks the end of wandering, of the nomadism of prehistoric man made possible by the mastery of breeding and agriculture. For the Greeks and Romans, when a home disappeared, it meant that the family had died out. These expressions have remained in the language and today we speak of the fiscal home and the risk of extinction of species.

The term *lustratio* evokes lustral water, water made sacred by the gesture of plunging a flaming brandle from the fireplace into the vase that contained it. The water screamed and quivered, bubbles bursting on its surface. As in wedding ceremonies, cakes made with flour flower were shared. Even today, on special occasions, we share bubbles and cookies.

A stable place to live is a home for the living who can more easily maintain the memory of the dead in a nearby burial ground. When the living live permanently in a *domus,* the dead also have a burial place close to the living and no longer at random in the nomadic life. Funerary monuments appear (the words "monument" and "memory" have the same etymology). In the Mediterranean region, in Corsica for example, it is still quite common to find domestic cemeteries on the family estate. The ritual celebrations of remembrance, on All Saints' Day for example, are always the occasion to light candles on these graves.

The charge of celebrating the *sacra privata*[13], the private rites of the memory of the dead were transmitted from generation to generation until complete extinction of the *familia* or the *people.* The son succeeded the father. When a *pater familias* had no children, he adopted a member of another family or another *gens,* so that the *sacra* of his family or his *gens* were not interrupted. Also the meaning of the adoption among the Greeks and the Romans was to perpetuate the *sacra,* when the *pater familias* had not had a son. In the absence of a son, a designated heir was to continue the office.

---

13. DAREMBERG (Charles), SAGLIO (Edmond), *Dictionnaire des Antiquités grecques et romaines d'après les textes et les monuments,* 10 volumes, Paris, Hachette, 1877-1919. See the article "sacra", vol. 4, p. 948-951.

From the very first days of life, the child is invited to perpetuate this cycle which must never be interrupted.

The *amphidromia* were the occasion to introduce the child to the ancestors but also to introduce the elders to the child. From this inter-generational dependence derives the reciprocal rights and duties that bind parents and children. In order for the child to one day honor the ancestors, the parents must protect the child until then. The belief of the primitive Greek and Roman family in the imperative need for the dead to be honored and nourished by the living, which is found in all civilizations, in order to continue their journey into the afterlife is probably no longer shared today in this form. But we still have the concern of the origins and the duty of memory which still mark deeply the psyche of each one, like unconscious legacies. The need to search for one's origins and the passion that is currently developing for genealogy are other good examples. Losing the link with one's roots remains a tragedy and emigration can be difficult for the second generation who no longer have contact with the grandparents' generation. Sometimes, "big brothers" are called upon to replace a lost ancestral link.

Children know that their function is to remember the old

This imperative need to cultivate the memory of the dead, but also to find support in it, marks little children much earlier and much more than we imagine. In a sanitized society that seeks to put death and the dead at a distance, I am always struck by the pathological grief of young children who become sad, worried, have trouble slee-ping and talk about the death of a family member they have never seen other than in a photo or in the story of the adults. Parents are surprised, "She didn't even know him, my grandfather died several years before she was born." Being depressed, worrying those around them with morbid talk about death, and questioning the final resting place of a missing family member is a good way to bring a missing person back to life. These children literally "mourn" an ancestor they believe to be forgotten and make it their mission to remind the living of his memory.

This mother in the maternity ward no longer had any elders to support her, and it was her duty to introduce the family's dead to the baby. This was imperative. On the occasion of the birth of this child, she had to occupy three functions at once: mother of her daughter, the dead to whom she could present her, and the elders on whom she could rely. Let the elders welcome the child and support the mother, and let the child be invited to honor her forefathers.

She was alone and had to fulfill all these functions in her role as *mater familias*. Mother, elders, forefathers. She broke down and only managed to introduce death to her baby. She started by taking the place of the dead.

But I was sitting there, between her and her baby. The visitor that I was probably took the place of the old and then occupied the place of the dead. I served as an ephemeral family prosthesis and faded into the shadows when I became unnecessary. It was in the aftermath, in the months that followed, as I listened to him tell me the story of his family, that I understood all this.

I was, without knowing it, the elders on whom the mother relied when I was present. I was the dead, to whom she wanted to introduce her daughter when I was no longer there.

Such is the transitory prosthetic function of the therapist who embodies the missing limb and then disappears when it is named: to make what is missing exist through the verb, to offer a signifying prosthesis to replace the missing link of memory.

A child is a connection between the dead and the living.

A visionary of the reality of intergenerational connections: Leonardo da Vinci

Leonardo da Vinci knew the principle of Russian dolls, the emotional connections of babies, and the connections from beyond the grave.

If you don't believe me, go to the Louvre.

The works of art of the most brilliant artists express the unspeakable and bring to light feelings that we would have difficulty in naming. We are not so much moved by the technical prowess of the artist - this is an indispensable condition - as because he has put it at the service of the expression of universal emotions that touch us without us being able to identify the sources. It is an aesthetic emotion that resonates in us without us knowing why. Leonardo da Vinci's painting, *The Virgin and Child with Saint Anne* (circa 1513), exhibited at the Louvre Museum, has this effect on me and makes me think of connected babies, Russian dolls and connections from beyond the grave.

A classical painting is certainly boring, you may say. But this one is as strange as our story of Russian dolls and a dead woman in childbirth, if you let yourself be penetrated by the scene. Three generations, the Virgin Mary, her mother, Saint Anne, and her son, the Child Jesus, are brought together in an unlikely place. High mountain peaks in the background, a precipice in the foreground. What are the three of them doing there on the edge of the abyss in this landscape of giants?

Surprising picture also because none of the characters is in the place where one would expect it. The grandmother is sitting on a rock, the mother is sitting on the grandmother's lap. As for the Infant Jesus, he is not installed in the lap of the Virgin as in almost all the maternities of all the museums in the world. He has slipped from his mother's lap, he has run away, he is even galloping. He is in danger.

Leonard puts action to it. The scene turns into a drama. If the grandmother looks after her daughter with a benevolent gaze, the latter is faced with the escape of the boy. The latter is about to ride a sheep that he holds firmly by both ears like young children hold the handlebars of their carrier. Sure that, gone as he is, he is going to fall into the nearby void! He is at the edge of the abyss, literally and figuratively. But his mother manages to catch him with both hands so that he doesn't fall further. And if the child, unaware of the death that awaits him, has engaged in a centrifugal and dangerous action, he has nevertheless turned his head in a centripetal movement towards his mother whose eyes he meets at the last moment. Will fall? Will not fall? She begged him with her eyes, that he would let himself be taken, that he would return to the safety of her lap. She has hooked him with her eyes, he hangs there in return, while the grandmother seems to say to her daughter: "Trust me! I am here! You'll be able to save him." The most stressed is the daughter.

Let's summarize. A grandmother carries her daughter on her lap - what a regression! -, who herself holds her child more or less deftly, who is in danger of falling into the void. Strange scenario!

What can we understand from this scene if not that this grand-mother, by her simple presence - she seems quite detached - gives enough confidence to her daughter for her to succeed in saving the child. The inner security given by the lived experience of a good emotional connection is transmitted from generation to generation, a mother can connect to her child and avoid death if the previous generation remains available and connected. Without electricity there is no connection. Without connection no safe baby.

The grandmother serves as a support for the mother who, in turn, holds the child with a look. Russian dolls nested in each other and connected. Leonardo's painting is built on this structure, the right arm of the grandmother merges with that of her daughter, the left arm of the Virgin is extended by that of the baby. It is a brilliant image of the system of Russian dolls and the phenomenon of emotionally connected babies, but also of the place of death and the dead around the birth of a child. The ancestors are present in the background, personified by the rocky peaks, a universal theme found in the monumental statues of the founding fathers of the Nation on Mount Rushmore in the United States. Remarkably, the Sioux used to call these rock towers "Six Grandfathers."

Death is the ravine.

Who can carry a mother carrying her baby?

Who can or must ensure the mother's support? It may well be the father - but also any other emotional support of the mother - who, summoned to this function of support, suddenly changes place and stature. He no longer plays the role of partner but embodies the function of protector, the one who supports the mother who carries the child. This has nothing to do with the psychologizing conceptions of the "third party" in the "mother-child" relationship that we are constantly told about, which lead to this ridiculous image of the father reduced to the role of a pruning shears obliged to cut the cord with a symbolic gesture like the mayor cuts a ribbon. As if the father or the companion of the mother or any other emotional support of this mother, had no other function than the insemination, the section of the cord and to become a co-educator. It is indeed to a quite other dimension that the one who embodies this affective support is called to reach, the mission to occupy a symbolic place in the succession of the generations by ensuring the carrying of the mother who carries the child.

10 - First glances, first links?

Recognize the child, recognize yourself in the child

At this point of our journey in the world of toddlers, you will have understood that a baby is not very concerned with his biological or legal filiation but rather seeks to choose stable and safe emotional boundaries, because his physical and psychological survival depends on it.

But what about the parents? Does a "pure biological child" carry within him or herself, by the grace of carrying the genes of his or her parents, the assurance that the parents will really love and recognize him or her as their own?

Does biological filiation offer the guarantee of a good investment of the child by its parents? The story of Elouan, a failed encounter between a mother and her child, already raised this question.

You all know stories from parents around you, perhaps you, who tell of the first meeting with their child, that first glance exchanged, which seals their bond forever. "Just after I gave birth, Ugo was taken to an incubator and we were separated for one night. But I met his eyes. I knew he was my child and I saw in his eyes that I was his mother."

Things are not always that simple

The first time that a mother came to consult me to evoke this question and to tell me her difficulty in recognizing herself in her baby, I tried to find explanations on the side of psychiatric theories, it was my training. But to my great astonishment, this mother who was there, in front of me, explaining to me that she only saw in her child a stranger, was neither depressed, nor delusional, nor more neurotic than anyone else. I also knew that the establishment of the mother-child bond could be damaged by the fact of a disjunction between the hoped-for child and the real child, a girl instead of a boy for example, a handicapped or sick child, or a child who arrived at the heart of a marital conflict. But here again, in this mother's case, none of these bad surprises that sometimes disturb the time of the mother-child meeting were present.

The very fact that she testified to this showed that she was not overwhelmed by neurotic guilt but rather was quite free with her words. Announcing that she did not want a child was already considered a suspicious choice, so daring to reveal that she had no feelings for a "natural" child that had been programmed and expected is much worse. To admit it is to show parental perjury because it is a real outrage to the social ideal of the family. In our cultural schemes, a mother cannot not love her child. This is also true for fathers.

So, this mother had come with her daughter of 3 years and a few months to tell me that she was forced to play the comedy of being a mother for almost three years. She did everything the way a mother should do, the way she imagined a mother should do, but she never felt any maternal emotion.

"It was an ordeal, an imposition, a sham, but I didn't know what it was to feel like a mother. Yet in the eyes of others I was. I saw myself distant from this child, I did not find myself in her. It was a secret that I could not tell anyone, not her father, not my mother, not my sister, and certainly not the pediatrician or my doctor. They wouldn't understand. This silence that I could not break made this feeling of imposture even worse. I felt that my maternal love was lying to my daughter and that I was deceiving others about my true feelings. But how could I admit such a thing. It was inconceivable. A mother has to be a mother. Everyone imagines that maternal love is written into the genes like the milky rise. That the feeling of being a mother begins with childbirth and overflows with hormones.

One day, she must have been almost 3 years old, we were in the kitchen, and Ludivine, that's her name, called me. She said "mom" to me as she said it twenty, thirty times a day and I turned around to answer her. Our eyes met and, believe it or not, at that moment, like St. Paul on the road to Damascus, I had the emotion of being a mother for the first time. Something indescribable, sweet and violent at the same time, overwhelmed me. I had tears in my eyes and I wanted to take her in my arms. It was the first time that this gesture and this emotion came from me, spontaneously. Before, when I took Ludivine in my arms, it was because she came to me and that I could not refuse her the gestures of tenderness that she was waiting for. But it was an intellectual response, not an emotion.

So you might say to me, if everything is fine now, why are you coming for a consultation today? It is no longer necessary! It is precisely because things are better that I want your advice: I am now much more concerned about my daughter's well-being. I now absolutely need to know if Ludivine has suffered from my emotional indifference. Before, I was unable to ask this question. Indeed, I would have been forced to confess what I felt was an infernal deception and that was impossible for me.

So what do you think of Ludivine?"

She was doing very well!

An isolated case?

A second mother who came to introduce me to her son explained:
"I admire parents who naturally love their children, I wish I felt the same way about my son.

Marc is 5 years old and his little sister just turned 4 months old. With this little girl my relationship was very different from the very first moment. I recognized her and I recognized myself in her right away. That never happened with Marc. It was this contrast that surprised and worried me.

My husband was on a mission in Africa and Marc was born there. He was the only white baby in the maternity ward. There was no risk of confusing him with anyone else, even though babies of color have darker skin at birth. Yet, when he was placed in my arms, we were like two strangers. This was clearly visible in the photo taken by his father at the time. Two strangers.

Yet it was a desired baby. But the installation of our relationship was strange. When he was born, nothing, I felt nothing. Or rather the fear of losing him. And the lack of desire to go to him. Both at the same time. It was paradoxical. Whenever I see him, I am afraid. I'm afraid he's sick and I'm afraid when he has a fever.

But when he needed something, I didn't even go to him to help or comfort him. I had no concern for him. If he forgot or lost his blanket, if he cried because he had lost it, I said, "It's okay, you'll find it!

I don't feel maternal with him, even though I am overflowing with sensitivity for my daughter.

The previous mother's old confidences about her "maternal conversion" led me to ask Marc's mother if a similar experience had happened to her.

"Did you ever, in those five years, feel a little more empathy for him with the feeling of a real encounter between the two of you, as you describe for your daughter?"

"There were never any good times. It's horrible to think that and even more horrible to say it. I have to admit that I suffered from having to take care of him. I saw myself leaving him in his playpen and not wanting to see him anymore. When he's sick, for a split second, the first thought that comes to mind is that he's only doing this to annoy me. I raised him, I did what I had to do - I tried to be a mother after all - but now that I've had this second baby, my daughter, she's 4 months old, I realize that it's completely different. She, it was obvious that she was my baby."

She stops talking, dries her eyes. Marc plays quietly in his corner without getting involved in the conversation. He steps aside and lets his mother vent. But in the small slice of silence which settles, he leaves the wooden toys on the carpet, takes his stuffed rabbit which he had abandoned on the ground and goes to deposit it carefully in the handbag of his mother while declaring:

"I'll leave my comforter in your bag so I don't forget it." And he goes back to his games.

She says she is not sure she recognizes him as her son, but he knows who his mother is. Fine, she still notices his gesture and adds:

"Sometimes I feel a little sorry for him. He can come up to me ten times, fifteen times in a row and say, 'Mommy, I love you,' like he's hoping to trigger something in me. But it doesn't do anything for me. He is probably looking for me to reassure him of my feelings for him. I find it hard to cuddle with him. I don't feel like it. In the maternity ward, physiologically he was my child, but emotionally or emotionally it wasn't obvious at all. To me, it was as if it wasn't mine. Or at least it was the logic, the reasoning that made me say it was mine, but not the heart."

Marc was in much more pain than Ludivine.

Yet another mother

"Matias was born premature and it was hard to bond with him. I felt like I was taking care of a child but that it wasn't my child. That this child was not mine. I was distractedly taking care of it, it was a task to be done. I was doing it, I was doing it well. But one day, I frightened myself. I had the feeling that I was taking care of someone else's child, a foreign child.

I get along very well with my mother-in-law! It happens! I explained to her that there was something wrong with Matias. I described to her how strange I thought my feelings were. That I cared for him well, or so I thought, but I had no empathy for him. It wasn't that easy to admit such difficulties to his mother-in-law. Imagine the imaginary projections, the gossip and the family fallout. She let me confide my questions to her. She didn't give me any specific answers that I remembered, but I felt heard. She did not judge me. On the contrary, I felt supported. A solidarity of mothers. Who can we allow to tell this kind of thing? And later, little by little, this feeling of emotional anaesthesia went away without me even realizing it. Today, it is my son. I don't know how it happened, but he's my son."

It is necessary to note there that the posture of this mother-in-law, by her respectful listening, not moralizing, which contains and supports, points out the principle of the Russian dolls.

These three mothers were neither depressed nor especially neurotic. They were not in a situation of family conflict or precariousness. Their babies were desired and expected, and did not themselves have any particular traits that might have been a handicap to their investment by their mothers.

Biological filiation is only a fiction

Wasn't this simply an expression of the now recognized fact that even in a biological birth, parents must adopt their child and the child must affiliate with its parents. And sometimes this is not automatic.

Mater certissima, pater semper incertus says the maxim. But since Dolly the sheep and especially since the birth of Louise Brown, the first test-tube baby, on July 26, 1978, the true nature of filiation has been revealed to humanity without us having yet fully understood it.

Fertilization is no longer a process enclosed in women's bodies, a reality that confuses the distinction between biological and psychological motherhood.

I challenge you today, out of confidence of course, to tell when you meet a couple with a child whether this child is the biological child born from their parents or a child born from a combination of exogenous gametes or from an embryo donation. And it doesn't matter anymore.

The myth of biological filiation has sunk with the progress of... biology. Men and women are now equal in this respect: they must all recognize that they must adopt their child from wherever it comes from. On a psychological level, biological filiation is only a fiction and biological truth is only a delusion.

The wonder of the talking newborn

To discover another illustration, I invite you to make a detour to the Louvre.

Benvenuto Tisi had a friend, Raphael, his *alter ego* in painting, whose way of painting was so close to his that their works were often confused. For some, it is said, only they knew the true author. Nevertheless, Benvenuto betrayed himself by reproducing on the back of his own paintings a carnation - *garofano* in Italian - reminding us of his nickname, Il Garofalo.

He was also the creator of a series of engravings, a kind of comic strip before its time, of which the Louvre Museum has three plates in its reserves. They were long attributed to his friend Raphael, wrongly. This set of three successive images tells the story of the miracle known as "the newborn child".

The story of this prodigy is as follows.

First panel, first scene: A jealous husband suspected his wife of having cheated on him and claimed that the child she had just given birth to was someone else's. She, offended and hurt, appealed to Saint Anthony of Padua who happened to be passing by. She, offended and hurt, appealed to Saint Anthony of Padua who was passing by just in time.

In front of the family and the assembled crowd, some people look serious, others feel sorry for her, she exposes her misfortune to the holy man. To show her affection, she puts her hand on the child's little arm.

"My good monk Anthony, my husband does not want to recognize my baby as his son because he claims that I have defiled his honor. Before Our Lord, I affirm that this child is his."

The paternal doubt

The baby is in the arms of the next woman and looks in turn at his mother, his putative father and Saint Anthony. This one then questions the husband.

"How about you?"

With an open hand placed over his heart as a sign of sincerity, the man replied:

"I am no longer a man in my prime and my vigor is no longer that of my twenties. It would be a great coincidence if this child were mine. Especially since my wife is still beautiful and young. I suspect some dashing youth to have sought to corrupt her.

Titian also painted this scene. He had added a character, a young man dressed in red, who was fidgeting behind the group, which suggests that this painter had the malice to give credit to this version.

But the man continued:

"In the face of this weakness that sometimes afflicts me, that takes away sleep from my nights and darkens my days, who could dissuade me from these thoughts?"

Saint Anthony did not want to go any further on this ground, which his vow of chastity forbade him to even think that it could exist, and asked that the newborn child be presented to him.

Saint Anthony in conciliation with a baby

Second plate.

The next one entrusts the child to Saint Anthony. The latter carries him on his arm and talks with the baby.

The father half turns away and now sketches with his hands a gesture of rejection expressing in advance his disbelief at anything that might happen at this crucial moment. "I have nothing to look forward to. What is the use of this at my age? From now on, nothing good can be granted to me" he said to himself. In his torment, he hasn't even bothered to take a look at this newborn baby since birth.

All the eyes of the spectators then converge on the two protagonists who are talking to each other in the center of the group. The scene is astonishing: Saint Anthony and the baby are in conciliation. In this second engraving the baby is represented as the real and only interlocutor of the holy man while the father is soliloquizing.

"Newborn child, by the Lord, I command you, reveal to us who your father is."

According to tradition, the child said, pointing to the grizzled man, "He is my father. But the truth is that Il Garofalo did not transcribe the dialogues, he concentrated on the succession of exchanges of looks and their effects.

A tenderized father

Third plate and last scene.

The child is back in his nurse's arms and is still holding his index finger up to his father and looking at him. The father has risen. A bright astonishment crosses his face. The mother kneels down. The saint blesses them.

This time, the father's hand is still on his heart, but almost folded, in a gesture of contrition, of submission too, and of recognition for sure. This child looked at him and he responded to that look. He was captivated by the insistent beauty of this child's gaze. This child, it is certain, is his son. Who would not want to be the father of such a child?

The extraordinary wonder of this miracle does not lie in the child's ability to speak, but in the demonstration that in the Italian Renaissance there was a genuine interest in observing the child, considered, at least in the arts, as a being in its own right. In this legend, Saint Anthony of Padua reveals in this newborn child his ability to awaken the feeling of fatherly love in his father, with a simple glance.

"That's my son."

And heaven, the saint and the audience submitted to this election.

Afterword: Taking into account the traumatic memory of babies and the psychological suffering of infants: a new frontier for our society

Some babies learn to protect themselves very quickly

Lorenzo, 1 month old, cries without sound.

- It was his father who shook him, because he cried.

- How old was he?

- He was 1 month old.

- What happened?

- It was morning. He should have not gotten up. He should have woken me up and not bothered. Lorenzo was crying. He was sleeping at the foot of our bed. He must have been hungry. So he shook him. He took him under his arms, he took him out of the cradle and he shook him. (The mother mimes a shaker movement with both hands. The father listens to the mother, nods in agreement, but frowns a little. He doesn't quite seem to agree).

- Oh, you're exaggerating, I didn't mean it. I just shook it a little, moved it a little.

- It was brutal! And you heard yourself yelling? You said, "I'm going to throw him down if he keeps yelling."

- Yeah! But that's when I get mad! That's okay!

- He shook it and his eyes went like this." (The mother mimes with her eyes going up to the ceiling, turning all white, eyelids fluttering and head falling back).

- It's like when you faint," adds the father, confirming the mother's words, but revealing his inability to understand the violence of her act and the seriousness of the trauma inflicted.

I am appalled.

- So, as you say, you stirred him up and he passed out.

- Oh yes! I had forgotten to put my hand behind his head to hold him, as the nursery nurse says. (He makes the gesture of holding a baby's head by putting his hand in a cup while his opposite arm pretends to support a small body).

- And then? (The mother speaks again.)

- I went to the PMI (Protection maternelle et infantile) in the morning. I had an appointment with the nursery nurse, so I took the opportunity to tell her about it. With the doctor, they told me to take her to the hospital. Fortunately there was no bleeding in his brain or eyes.

- Your baby loses consciousness and you haven't even called the doctor or the ambulance?

- But I protected him Lorenzo, I went there. I protected him, that's what they told me at the PMI.

- In a way, yes. You have protected him from much worse.

- You see, you also say that I protected him. (Lorenzo's mother pauses.) I protected him but maybe not enough.

Following his mother's statements, Lorenzo was placed by the prosecutor in the nursery after a short hospitalization. The medical examinations did not reveal any brain damage, which was a great opportunity[14] .

A baby keeps memories of trauma

Lorenzo arrived in the ward at 4 weeks old. He was a baby who stood in a ball and had the wrinkled face of a little old man. A baby bird fallen from the nest, with a serious and grave expression. Instead of meeting the eyes of his mothering mothers, he would stare at a point above their foreheads, at the edge of the hair. If you managed to meet his eyes, his gaze would cross you without giving the impression that he had seen you. And never a smile. Trying to talk to him and get his attention didn't seem to provoke any interest from him. But for the first week he could only fall asleep when he was in his arms.

He wasn't crying, or more accurately, you couldn't hear him cry. They were sobs without the sound. When he couldn't contain himself, he let out a little hiccuping noise that irritated his throat, like an old car that had trouble starting and whose battery had also had some weakness. Lorenzo held back his tears. Less than a month old, he understood the danger of making noise. Although his parents had only mentioned a single event, Lorenzo's reactions suggested that he had probably been abused several times, to the point where he had learned to avoid crying.

---

14. A baby who is not yet able to hold his head must be handled with care because of his muscular weakness. Shaking a baby can simply kill him or leave him permanently disabled by causing irreversible brain damage. Simultaneous hemorrhages of the brain and retina, characteristic of these traumas, have been described in infants since the beginning of the 20TH century. The cause was unknown at the time. It was not until 1972 that an American pediatrician and radiologist, John Caffey, reported them as the consequences of a violent shaking of the child...

The prosecutor allowed the parents to visit Lorenzo several times a week. We never left them alone with the baby. His father did not try to take care of him, but he was the only person whose gaze this child was looking at. From Lorenzo it was not a questioning, discovering, greeting or inviting look, but a hypnotic look that shone with extreme vigilance and made one very uncomfortable. It was incongruous to see such a young baby looking at an adult with such a stare. An infant has few expressions at his disposal because his range of facial expressions is insufficient to convey the variety of his emotions. They can only be guessed in his eyes.

Lorenzo was a very limp baby who had no muscular strength, except when his father picked him up. When his father lifted him under his arms, with careless gestures, raising him upright like a vase being raised, Lorenzo held his head. He contracted his whole body in a gesture of self-protection when he was so soft the rest of the time. Lorenzo, who usually did not meet anyone's eyes and was completely amorphous, was now staring at his father, eyes in eyes, and contracting between the hands that held him. At the very beginning of his reception, before he managed to relax, the nursery nurses had noticed that he remained fearful during the care and thus stiffened at the undressing, clenched fists, arms stuck along the body, his face shriveled, his features hard and crumpled.

As for his mother, she seemed helpless, awkward in her gestures, uncomfortable. Her ill-adapted attitude with her baby at the maternity hospital - when he cried, the nursery nurse had to recommend that she hold him against her - had motivated the planning of a visit by the nursery nurse to Lorenzo's home every 15 days. During this meeting the mother expressed many complaints: "Lorenzo cries too much, he doesn't calm down. He doesn't like the bath, he cries too. I give him as little as possible, I am afraid he will drink the cup."

Lorenzo then began to cry. As this continued, the nurse offered to try to take him and the mother was surprised that he had calmed down so quickly in unknown arms. The nursery nurse, not very familiar with the phenomenon of selective connections of babies, was surprised by this observation and remained doubtful about the reality of the difficulties alleged by the mother. She was unable to conceive that she, a professional, a stranger to the family, could be more reassuring for this baby than his own mother... If this baby calms down so well in my arms, it is because he is confident, confident in the humans that he could only acquire from his mother, therefore this mother exaggerates his difficulties or in any case the baby does not suffer from them and everything is reassuring... The future was going to disprove this reasoning, which is certainly benevolent but angelic.

Crying without fear

In the nursery, with his educators, Lorenzo understood little by little, in a few weeks, that he could cry without fear. At first it was only a little shy cry, but a real baby cry, very different from the restrained hiccups he had been used to. The first time, his mother was astonished to discover that it was Lorenzo who had produced this discreet little calling sound, which was addressed to him and was appropriate to the circumstances. She was busy welcoming a couple, a foster family, who were coming to meet the baby who would soon be coming to their home. Desperate to wait, Lorenzo had dared to make himself heard. She was very upset.

It was only gradually that he gave up his stress and managed to relax in the arms of his educators. Carrying Lorenzo became easier, he felt less like he was supporting an inert body. He was still not smiling, but he was no longer consistently running away from the eyes that were on him. Some unhealthy babies stare at your eye but don't look at you. Lorenzo was beginning to accept a penetrating gaze.

In the following months, his positive evolution was confirmed. Lorenzo became over time a charming baby, well in exchange, with harmonious relationships. A beautiful little boy too.

But the body care was still marked by great anxiety and he was still very vigilant and tense. He was very sensitive to words and very good at listening. At about 6 months of age, a small lung infection forced our pediatrician to prescribe a few sessions of respiratory physiotherapy, an effective but uncomfortable technique. Babies cry a lot. But Lorenzo, lying on the table, remained stiff and contracted, holding back his tears while the physiotherapist patted his back. The nursery nurse who had stayed by his side saw him pleading for her gaze. Then she said to him:

"You can cry Lorenzo, I know it's unpleasant."

Lorenzo looked at her, grieving, then let go of all his tension and finally allowed himself to cry loudly, with tears, which is not so bad to clear the airways.

Adults forget, the baby remembers

His relationship with his parents remained marked by a strong anxiety that manifested itself both in avoiding contact with them and in seeking support from professionals.

Lorenzo is 3 months old. At the parental visit, he is in his baby carriage and his mother tries to get him to smile. No answer, she insists. Unlucky, Lorenzo runs away from her and refuses to look at her. She is exasperated. Instead of calming down, of waiting, of trying to tame him, of letting him come, she picks him up and takes him out of this protective shell. She carries it in the arms like a trophy but there is no complicity between them.

A month and a half later. This time the visit is accompanied by an educator whom Lorenzo does not know well. His parents are waiting in their chairs. The educator crouches down and carries Lorenzo so that he is at their level. The mother reaches out to pick him up but Lorenzo stiffens. The educator keeps Lorenzo in her arms and suggests that everyone take their time to be together. Lorenzo ends up smiling and chatting while looking at his mom and dad. The educator then allows herself to entrust Lorenzo to his mother, but he is riveted to her gaze rather than being in conversation with his mother. Annoyed, she tries a ploy to get Lorenzo to take his eyes off her and cling to his parents.

"Address your little boy to maintain the relationship with him while I walk behind you to get me a chair."

And instead of taking a close one, she goes around the parents by the back, thinking to get away from Lorenzo's adhesive look.

But Lorenzo followed her with his eyes all the way around, craning his neck to the point that Dad remarked:

"Even while doing this, he's still looking at you."

Lorenzo's story shows us that babies retain memories of the trauma they have experienced and the identity of their abuser. They also quickly identify who they can feel safe with. Here are two other examples involving very young babies.

Amélie is taken of a violent dizziness

Amélie was severely abused by her delusional mother after leaving the maternity ward. She had several broken limbs and her skull. She came out of it by miracle. After three weeks in intensive care she was placed in the nursery at the age of one month. She was a very tense baby. She rarely unclenched her little fists, refused any visual encounter with her mothering staff, but was very alert to everything that was happening around her. She was on the alert, always on the lookout, trusting no one so much that she never quite closed her eyes to sleep. The educators had to tame her gently. After two months of very attentive mothering, the least invasive possible, all in delicacy, Amélie began to be reassured a little. She now accepted to meet the eyes of the educators, but in a furtive way. She then began to try a few discreet smiles. If she still looked serious and remained distant most of the time, the progress was visible. It was confirmed over the next few months. The emotional connection with the humans began again.

Her mother obtained visiting rights shortly after Amélie's arrival at the nursery and their relationship, instead of following the positive evolution of this little girl, only worsened over time. In the first period, her mother took her in her arms but did not speak to her, did not address her. Amélie was very tense and could not look at her mother. As the visits continued in the same way, the little girl began to cry in her mother's arms for no apparent reason. These cries increased from week to week and only stopped when her mother put her in the stroller and just talked to her from a distance.

An appointment with my child psychiatrist colleague took on a particularly dramatic dimension. Amélie was crying with heartbreaking cries as her mother recounted what had happened during the severe abuse. Suddenly she stopped, looked at her mother with intensity, and then turned her head in one go. Her eyes then began to show intense nystagmus - involuntary, rapid, jerky movements of the eyeballs - which was probably the result of a violent dizziness. My colleague had to stroke her head and talk to her to reassure her that she was there for it to subside.

Jasmina: One! Two! Three! Danger!

Jasmina, who arrived at the nursery at 4 months old, had learned to keep quiet before her mother finished counting: One! Two! Three! It's impossible to know if she had memorized the verbal sequence announcing the worst, if she had spotted her mother's aggressive tone or even visualized the threatening features of her face. In any case, she was crying when the terrifying countdown began. Her mother explained it to us, very proud of this great educational achievement in front of what she called Jasmina's caprices and that, according to her, the little one would have started to show from the age of 1 month. During a parental visit, she wanted to demonstrate this to us in front of the beginning but still discreet cries of her daughter: "Don't cry Jasmina!" still conciliating but already insistent.

Then: "Jasmina! Don't cry!" in an imperative tone before starting her terrible countdown. But in front of the astonished look of the accompanying person, she stopped that day at the number two.

And how many babies have we received who had been used as human shields in scenes of domestic violence or as hostages promised to be thrown out the window if the "other" threatened to leave. Babies who are involved in the most direct conjugal violence present early, severe and long-lasting post-traumatic syndromes, characterized by a major insecurity and an impressive anxious reactivity in situations of loud noises, raised voices or when faced with unknown faces.

Keeping quiet to survive

It can be hard to admit that babies as young as a few weeks old are able to hold back their crying to avoid even worse. It took me a decade of working with these babies for this phenomenon to become obvious and familiar to me and to our entire nursery team. The accumulation of repeated and consistent observations convinced us of this reality. Babies can feel hunger, thirst, the cold of a wet diaper, the discomfort of an irritating bowel movement, the anxiety of the evening, the distress of not being cradled in the lap of supportive arms, the pain of colic, the discomfort of being too hot, and all the little and big inconveniences of the life of a baby who can't do anything on his own, babies can feel all of this without showing anything. They are able to keep quiet to limit the risk of being mistreated, which they have experienced before and several times to the point of being able to integrate the notion of danger and the way to avoid it. It can be by simple anxious stupefaction, like a prey simulating inanition to divert the attention of a predator, or by pure imitation of the basic reflex of animals who, with their defenses weakened, suffer in silence to avoid the risk of being spotted by predators. A baby who keeps quiet is a baby in danger. A big bawling baby who calms down quickly in the arms is much more reassuring than a little bird who doesn't say anything anymore.

Ancient experiments on the art of silencing babies

Silencing an infant through terror was a proven technique described by a famous Leipzig physician, Dr. Daniel Gottlieb Moritz Schreber (1808-1861).

Dr. Daniel Gottlieb Moritz Schreber wrote more than a dozen works on pedagogy, including a kind of guide for the education of children published in 1858[15] . He detailed an educational theory of absolute rigor that he applied to his own children. This very coercive, even totalitarian method had a large audience in Germany for more than a century and was able to participate in the development of Nazi ideas. Its principle was to break down any hint of personal autonomy in the child, from a very young age, and to obtain absolute and definitive obedience.

In this frightening literature one can read this advice for the child's first year: "If one is assured that there is no real need or anything that worries or hurts them, and that they are not ill, one can be convinced that the cries simply betray the expression of a mood, a caprice, their first voluntary manifestation... One must then intervene in a decisive manner: quickly distract the child's attention, talk to him sternly, threaten him with a gesture, hit him against his bed... or, if all this does not help, use moderate corrections, intermittent, repeated with logic, until the child calms down or falls asleep.

Such a procedure is only necessary once or twice, and the child is mastered forever[16]."

---

15. SCHREBER (Daniel Gottlieb Moritz), *Kallipädie oder Erziehung zur Schönheit durch naturgetreue und gleichmässige Förderung normaler Körper bildung,* Leipzig, Fleischer, 1858.
16. Quoted *in* SCHATZMAN (Morton), *L'Esprit assassiné* (1972), Paris, Stock, 1974.

And these were not just stated principles. They were applied with the utmost severity, as the anecdote told by this dangerous doctor testifies: "I will cite an incident that occurred in my own family. The nanny of one of my children, a very docile person, had given him - in spite of my formal prohibition - something to eat between meals: a slice of the pear that she herself was eating. For this reason alone, I sent her away immediately, since I could no longer expect unconditional loyalty from her." The news spread through Leipzig and "we never had such trouble with our staff again."

How to reign by terror on an infant, in one or two coercive and targeted sessions. And to separate him brutally from his affective attachment figure that must have represented this nurse who had a normal and human solicitude for this child: she shared with him his gustatory emotions and thus probably all the others.

Terror makes you crazy, Freud and Lacan saw nothing but fire

It is worth adding that his two sons went mad. Daniel Paul Schreber, president of the Dresden Court of Appeal, was hospitalized for several years and his brother Daniel Gustav committed suicide. The story of the persecutions experienced as a child by Daniel Paul Schreber, the famous author of *Memoirs of a Neuropath*[17], remained unknown until the publication of *The Murdered Mind*, a book by the American psychiatrist Morton Schatzman, who drew on recent historical and documentary research[18], revealing and detailing the educational fanaticism of Dr. Schreber, the magistrate's father. Morton Schatzman has established a direct, almost literal, link between the abuse of Daniel Paul Schreber as a child, the onset of

---

17. SCHREBER (Daniel Paul), *Memoirs of a neuropath*, Paris, Éditions du Seuil, coll. "Points Essais, 1995.
18. In particular on those of William G. Niederland, diffused from 1959.

161

his mental illness and the content of his delusions. He sheds new light on this work, an essential work in which Schreber Jr. relates his illness and whose reading provided Bleuler, Freud[19], Lacan[20], and so many others, with an incomparable model for the study of paranoia and schizophrenia. Generations of psychiatrists and psychologists have read it without knowing the details of its author's childhood.

Sigmund Freud made no connection between Schreber's father's extreme pedagogical ideas and his son's mental illness. Did he know about it? In any case, Freud held Schreber's father's work in high esteem, since he wrote about him in the introduction to his text "President Schreber: A Case of Paranoia" published in *Five Psychoanalyses* in 1907: "He was not an unimportant personality [...]. His activities to promote a harmonious education of the young, to ensure the coordination between home and school, to introduce physical culture and manual work in order to raise the level of health, all of this had an influence on his contemporaries. Indeed, the outdoor activity societies, created at the initiative of Dr. Schreber, lasted in Germany for more than a century and had several million members.

Lacan, in his 1955-1956 seminar on psychoses, where he relies on the text of Daniel Paul Schreber and on the commentary made by Freud, had the intuition of the risk of the outbreak of a psychosis in children confronted with the crushing personality of a father. But he did not go to the end of the demonstration that remained to be made between the early mistreatment of the child and its psychotic effect, and this, in a more certain way, the younger the child. Lacan nevertheless explains[21]: "We have all known these delinquent or psychotic sons who proliferate in the shadow of a paternal personality [...] in

---

19. FREUD (Sigmund) *Cinq psychanalyses*, Paris, Presses universitaires de France (PUF), 1993.
20. LACAN (Jacques), *The Seminar, book III, The Psychoses, (1955-1956)*, text established by Jacques-Alain Miller, Paris, Éditions du Seuil, 1981.
21. LACAN (Jacques), *The Seminar, book III, The Psychoses, (1955-1956)*, op. cit, loc. cit, p. 230.

the register of an unbridled ambition or authoritarianism [...]. It is not necessary that there be genius, merit, mediocre or bad, it is enough that there be unilateral[22] and monstrous. It is certainly not by chance that a psychopathological subversion of the personality occurs especially in such a situation."

A clinician of genius, trained through observation of separated babies

The same year, Jenny Aubry, more lucid, wrote[23] : "The quality of maternal care received by the child before separation is the essential factor in the nascent structuring of the personality. Several children hospitalized at Parent-de-Rosan spent the first months of their lives with mothers suffering from serious mental disorders before

---

22. This term of unilateral must be understood in reference to the clinic of psychosis that Lacan constructed as a counterpoint to that of neurosis. In the neurosis "the transmitter receives from the receiver his own message in inverted form". There is thus dialectic and exchange, mirroring and bilaterality. For the psychotic, his delusion, which is not an addressed message, does not require a dialectical exchange, a validation, an assent or a return of the other. His delusion is certain, it is the truth, one, whole. With this term of unilateral Lacan does not indicate that the father figures he evokes would be psychotic - they are not delusional and their message can be addressed - but that their discourse would be precisely one-sided - unilateral - and in this sense monstrous because it has no consideration for any otherness of the child, reducing him to a living being without recognized identity. "The subject then adopts this intimidated position that we observe in the fish or the lizard" he adds.

23. AUBRY (Jenny), *La Carence de soins maternels : les effets de la séparation et la privation de soins maternels sur le développement des jeunes enfants*, Paris, Presses universitaires de France (PUF),1955, *loc. cit.* p. 124. This book has now become a rare find, and yet, by an incredible chance, I discovered, misplaced in a bookshop, the copy that Dr. Jenny Aubry had personally dedicated to Professor Michel Soulé, a precursor of child psychiatry who had begun his career with separated children in the Assistance Publique in 1955. I keep this book as a precious heritage.

undergoing multiple changes and a serious lack of maternal care. Their psychic structure is neither atrophied as in cases of absence of maternal care, nor arrested in its development as in cases of late separation, but rather disintegrated and chaotic. Some will say that these children born of demented mothers are such because of their heredity; but without denying the psychic fragility of these children, what we have observed by studying their evolution and their reactions during the treatment incites us to think that the abnormal behaviors of the mother towards her child play a preponderant role in the formation of the psychosis..."

And on the infant's memory of possible abuse, she adds:

"... During the treatment, while Monique develops physically, the rites of an obsessive nature which protect her against this anguish multiply and are organized. It is necessary that during dramatic sessions she re-enacts the scenes of the first weeks of her life when her mother smothered her by feeding her and that she destroys by crushing a symbolic doll of herself so that gradually she can leave this state and rebuild a normal "self".

Conclusion: A plea for the recognition of the baby's psychic pain

Let's draw a parallel with the recent history of awareness of the effects of physical pain[24] in babies.

The recognition and consideration of physical pain in newborns and small children is a recent phenomenon. Twenty-five years ago, babies were operated on without anesthesia. Indeed, until the work of Anand, an anesthesiologist and pediatric resuscitator of Indian origin, at the end of the 1980s, the medical community considered the newborn to be insensitive to pain or at least incapable of integrating it and remembering it. Until that time, doctors did not consider pain to be something that would leave a mark on the child. Painful medical care and surgical interventions were done without analgesics, only under curare to avoid any risk of muscular defense and movement during the surgical act. The non-closure of the ductus arteriosus at birth, a frequent vascular anomaly of the aorta in babies,

---

24. I have chosen to use the term "physical pain" for the sake of clarity, but this word is subject to debate. The concept of nociception, or perception of painful impulses, describes the metabolic and neurobehavioral effects of noxious stimulation, regardless of any consideration of higher consciousness, memory, possible emotional effects, or induced psychic suffering. In fact, studies on newborn pain investigate and measure, directly or indirectly, nociception without concern for its cortical integration.

requires its ligation and, to do so, to open the thorax between two ribs and to place a clip in contact with the heart. Before Anand's work, this operation was performed without anesthesia. That was just over twenty years ago. Today it would seem horrible and barbaric.

Anand was able to demonstrate that the baby was not only sensitive to pain but had no neurological or cognitive means of filtering and controlling painful impulses. The younger the baby, the more sensitive he is to pain. This is even more pronounced if he is premature. Repeated pain makes him hyperalgesic, that is to say that a pain of the same intensity will provoke a stronger and longer lasting sensation at each new reappearance. The more pain the baby has experienced, the more reactive he will be to the pain.

Anand also introduced, which has now become obvious, that if the baby is unable to express that he is in pain, it is up to the observer to actively look for the signs of the manifestation of this pain. Today, there are pain assessment scales for infants, used in pediatric services, which are based on precise observation of facial expressions, crying or crying and the child's overall behavior. It is important to know that the most intense pain can cause a coma vigil, that is to say, a baby who is totally limp and unresponsive but who keeps his eyes open. This can give the illusion that the child is not feeling anything.

Pets, too, have no way of expressing their pain when they are sick. Most of the time, they are silent and hide in a corner. But since Anand's work, they have also benefited from the dissemination of these methods of pain observation and treatment. Veterinarians have noted, since they have been treating animal pain, that the aftermath of surgical interventions has been significantly improved, regardless of any philosophical or ethical considerations. The same observation has been made in human babies, for whom pain sedation prevents many of the postoperative complications that appeared before the use of analgesic treatments.

Thanks to the publication of these scientific articles, it is now recognized and admitted that letting a baby suffer is harmful and dangerous for its immediate and future health. It is also a gesture of humanity.

An identical intellectual revolution is necessary today so that the psychic pain, the psychological suffering of the babies subjected to deleterious affective conditions, and the devastating effects which result from it on their psycho-affective development are recognized. If observers are not convinced of the reality of psychic pain in babies, caused by trauma, affective insecurity, anarchy and chaos in the responses to their affective and vital needs, discontinuity of psychic carrying or vital distress, they will not recognize its manifestations and will misinterpret the behaviors of the baby and his parents.

The worst are those babies who are sticky, clinging, and have strong emotional demands on professionals, which reassures them, but is a sign of seriousness, like a drowning baby frantically clinging to his or her life preserver. At the other end of the spectrum are babies who have become amorphous and no longer even complain. These ones don't bother anyone. Babies who are as quiet as pictures.

Not taking this into consideration exposes the infant to the same complications as with physical pain. The younger the child is, the more sensitive he is to it, because it is his vital security that is endangered. These are therefore absolute psychological or child psychiatric emergencies. When the psychological pains are repeated, the baby becomes hyperesthetic before sinking into devastating psychological suffering. This condition leads to severe developmental delays, personality disintegration, and the destruction of the child's attachment skills.

As with physical pain, it is essential that childcare professionals learn to recognize its manifestations, which means that they must be trained to look for its expressions, which are delicate and subtle in a baby. The more serious the disorders are, the less visible they will be, because the child who is too damaged no longer struggles, like the painful child in a coma vigil, and no longer manifests himself. Remember Melanie, Lorenzo, Eric and the others.

The widespread idea of a certain fatality in the repetition of misfortunes from generation to generation in certain problem families is only a cowardice of thought and a failure of solidarity in our society.

Many babies and very young children subjected to unworthy living conditions and confronted with destructive emotional conditions could be saved from a dark future marked by personality, development and adaptation disorders, if our society would put the necessary human means to detect and take care of them before these irreversible damages appear. Over the past twenty-five years, immense progress has been made in the consideration and management of the physical pain of infants; the opposite would shock us today. The same revolution remains to be made in order to implement efficient tools to detect and take care of babies in psychological danger before they are destroyed.

It is a real public health problem but also a simple question of human solidarity towards our little fellow human beings.

A new challenge for social and care services but also a new frontier for our society.

ACKNOWLEDGEMENTS

This book would not have existed without the numerous intellectual and friendly collaborations with my colleagues from Angers over the last two decades. The writing of this book has been the occasion to renew rich and sustained exchanges with many of them and with specialists from other disciplines who have accepted to bring me criticism and light. It was an opportunity for discussions enlightened by a shared passion for the clinical observation of babies, our teachers in humanity, because our masters in emotions.

I can't name them all, but I would like to thank in particular :

Mireille R.

Lucie B.

Vladia C.

Daniele C.

Anita C.

Elisabeth R.

Marie-Noëlle L.

Astrid C.

Aurore S.

Christine L.

and the whole team of the Saint-Exupéry nursery in Angers

Not to mention :

Katia N., psychologist at the CHU of Angers

Gérard Lahouati, great specialist of Casanova

and the veterinary doctor Mandoline Chesnel for her advice on animal pain.

My thanks also go to Professor Véronique Dasen of the University of Fribourg and to Professor Jean-Bernard Garré of the Faculty of Medicine of Angers for their precious help concerning certain historical references (chapter 7).

Table of Contents

Table of contents

www.ingramcontent.com/pod-product-compliance
Lightning Source LLC
La Vergne TN
LVHW051157060726
842526LV00014B/3246